WordPerfect® Certification Success Guide

WordPerfect® Certification Success Guide

Brian Ford
Debra Kiefer-Ford

Windcrest®/ McGraw-Hill
New York San Francisco Washington, D.C. Auckland Bogotá
Caracas Lisbon London Madrid Mexico City Milan
Montreal New Delhi San Juan Singapore
Sydney Tokyo Toronto

Published by Windcrest, an imprint of McGraw-Hill, Inc.
The name "Windcrest" is a registered trademark of McGraw-Hill, Inc.

pbk 1 2 3 4 5 6 7 8 9 0 FGR/FGR 9 9 8 7 6 5 4
hc 1 2 3 4 5 6 7 8 9 0 FGR/FGR 9 9 8 7 6 5 4

Library of Congress Cataloging-in-Publication Data

Ford, Brian, 1960–
WordPerfect certification success guide / by Brian Ford and Debra Kiefer-Ford.
p. cm.
Includes index.
ISBN 0-07-021519-7 (pbk.)
1. WordPerfect (Computer file) 2. Word processing. I. Kiefer-Ford, Debra. II. Title.
Z52.5.W65F66 1994
652.5'536—dc20 94-34290
CIP

Acquisitions editor: Brad Schepp
Executive editor: Robert E. Ostrander
Production team: Katherine G. Brown, Director
Rhonda E. Baker, Coding
Wanda S. Ditch, Desktop Operator
Linda L. King, Proofreading
Jodi L. Tyler, Indexer
Designer: Jaclyn J. Boone

0215197
WK2

We would like to dedicate this book to our families and friends for their help and understanding during the writing process. Their encouragement during the process was invaluable.

We would also like to dedicate the book to our nephews Daniel and Russell, who are a constant source of energy and inspiration.

So much changed in our lives as we wrote this book that we would like to dedicate the book to the future.

Contents

Part 2
Examination guidance

Part 3
How to use your certification

Acknowledgments

The authors would like to acknowledge the contribution of many WordPerfect Corporation employees who helped us as we created this book.

We would especially thank Gary Ashton, director of certification at WordPerfect Corporation. Gary is a tireless evangelist for the WordPerfect certification program. We and WordPerfect Corporation owe much of this book to his vision.

We'd also like to thank the people of the certification department including Brad Van Alfen, Camie Jo Clark, and Linda Luck, who were always courteous, kind, and helpful.

The authors would also like to acknowledge the support of our families during the writing process.

Finally, we would like to thank Len Dorfman, Brad Schepp, and the people of Windcrest/McGraw-Hill, Inc.

Introduction

The *WordPerfect Certification Success Guide* is a resource for people seeking WordPerfect Corporation certification. Many people might find the process of becoming certified very difficult. Certification is not something that can be achieved by just anyone. It requires hard work and the development of not just knowledge but expertise with a software product. If you've picked up this book, then the idea of being recognized by WordPerfect Corporation and holding certification credentials to better your career, or perhaps starting a new career, is of importance to you.

This book is broken into four parts that help the reader make the decision to pursue certification, prepare for the test, fully utilize certification, and practice for tests. If you are interested in what certification is and want to understand why it is offered, read chapters 1–3 in part 1. If you want to become certified, part 2 (chapters 4–6) will help you move through the process of achieving certification. When you have been certified, part 3 includes some of our best ideas and tips for using certification to advance your career (chapters 7–9). Part 4 includes sample tests with answers separated from the respective questions to better simulate a test and not compromise the opportunity to learn by knowing the correct answer.

Appendix A is a collection of checklists to help you keep track of crucial elements of certification studies. Appendix B is a telephone directory of important resources for certification professionals; please realize that the telephone numbers are subject to change. The glossary is a guide to common terminology that you hear and will use.

In short, we have written this book as a guide for people traveling along the "certification expressway."

While we were writing this book about the WordPerfect certification program, it was announced that WordPerfect would be purchased by Novell, a large local area networking (LAN) operating system manufacturer. WordPerfect is now the cornerstone of the Novell Application Products Group. Perhaps the most profound change was the renaming of the WordPerfect Office product to Novell GroupWise. Where there were other changes, and there were not many, we've included notes about the merger.

We hope this book will answer your questions about WordPerfect certification. In writing this book, the authors have spoken to people at WordPerfect Corporation, people who hold WordPerfect certifications, and others who have been interested in the program. Here are some of the questions that we have been asked most often.

"Is it hard to get certified?"

Certification is a credential well respected in the computer industry. The WordPerfect program has been structured in such a way as to ensure that people who are certified demonstrate more than competence, but also expertise with the product.

Most certification programs offered by hardware or software manufacturers are targeted at the people who sell, install, maintain, and support the users of the manufacturers's product. WordPerfect Corporation's program started the same way, targeting those same people. This left people who use the product with no way of "proving" that they knew it very well.

As costs in the software industry have risen and more and more products are sold, dominant software companies have found it difficult to keep the customers satisfied despite all the "certified" installation and support people. More people are needed to support the products. The problem is that to get more people certified quickly, the company has to lower its certification standards. And when the standards are lowered, many of these new "certified" installation and support people can't keep customers satisfied.

WordPerfect has addressed this problem by setting a standard. It developed a model certification test that support people must pass. In order to prove the concept, WordPerfect created a test and gave the test to the people who support the product now, namely WordPerfect support employees. This helped the company identify what was a good question and what was a bad question.

But then WordPerfect did something else. The test was given to people who didn't know very much at all about WordPerfect's products. If the test was fair, then people who don't know WordPerfect should have done very poorly. If the pool of people that knew little about the program were able to "guess" correctly too often on one question, that question was either removed or rewritten.

What evolved is a computer-based test that could take up to 2 hours to complete. All the questions are multiple-choice, or multi-multiple-choice. Multiple-choice questions typically have one correct answer. Multi-multiple choice questions ask the person taking the test to pick all the correct answers from a series of options. Multi-multiple-choice questions are useful for testing troubleshooting skills to determine if the person taking the test knows more than one way to solve a problem.

It is important to understand that not everyone who becomes certified will have to take the same exam. There are different certification tests at different certification levels. Each level has different requirements and tests.

The WordPerfect certification test truly identifies people that can demonstrate expertise in solving business-related problems using WordPerfect products. Many people who have made their careers by "generalizing," or knowing several different competitors' programs

fairly well, probably will not be able to pass the WordPerfect certification exam.

It is important to realize that "certification" is a kind of a title. A title gives others some indication as to what the person is supposed to do. It does not necessarily mean that this person is good at doing what they do, but that they can do it. Becoming a WordPerfect Certified Professional, or Certified Instructor, or Certified Systems Engineer will tell people that you met established requirements to become certified.

"Will it be expensive?"

The WordPerfect program has been structured in such a way as to offer different preparation choices depending on the level of certification you seek to attain, the amount of time you want to spend preparing, and the computer and software resources you have available.

Classes are available from training centers across the United States, Canada, and worldwide that can quickly help a candidate prepare for the exam. If the candidate is employed at a company that already has the software installed and in use, a courseware kit may be purchased. WordPerfect has also created a new program that will allow colleges, universities, technical schools, and adult education programs to offer classes leading to certification.

A popular variation on the question of cost was *"Do I have to own a computer?"* or *"Do I have to own a copy of WordPerfect?"* While WordPerfect Corporation would like everyone to own a copy of the product, there is no requirement to supply a software license number or other proof of ownership before you are certified. Although owning the appropriate hardware and software is not a requirement, it is very beneficial.

"But what if I'm just a user?"

WordPerfect's certification program recognizes that not everyone is a software trainer or consultant; therefore, a certification category intended for advanced users of their products is offered. This idea of certifying users' skills is something that makes the WordPerfect program different from that of many other companies.

There is no requirement that you have prior computer experience or hold a computer degree from an educational institution. It is necessary that you have knowledge of how to use a DOS computer and perform several basic tasks.

"Will I have to go to WordPerfect Corporation to get certified?"

Unlike other companies' certification efforts, WordPerfect does not require certification candidates to take a course directly from WordPerfect Corporation. The certification exams that candidates need to pass to become certified are offered by third-party testing companies. These testing companies have stated that in most cases no candidate should have to travel more than an hour from his or her home to take a certification exam.

"Why is there a certification program?"

Until recently, WordPerfect offered toll-free telephone support to all users of its products. Even when WordPerfect Corporation was providing free support, it started and maintained a certification program. The reason for creating and sustaining the certification program was to ensure the high quality and level of service that certified support and training companies offered to WordPerfect Corporation clients.

Certification by WordPerfect Corporation is even more important today, given that the company no longer provides toll-free telephone support at no-charge. This policy change to charge customers for support after a period of time will drive many customers to seek out local professionals for support and training services.

Content overview

The WordPerfect certification program includes several different products and offers different levels of certification for each product.

This book will explain each of these different products and the certifications that can be attained. We will tell you about what the requirements and the benefits are for each program.

As authors, we've tried to make this book different from many of the other titles available about certification. We are both certified; we realize that there is no "easy way" to get certified.

This book will not teach you how to use any WordPerfect product. There are dozens of books and hundreds of classes that can do that. Rather than try to tell you about all the possible test questions that you could be asked, this book will try to help you understand how the tests are developed. We did this so that the readers could develop their own test questions. We will help you develop a personal plan to prepare for a test, take the test, and pass.

Once you have achieved certification, we will give you ideas about how to use it to your best advantage. Support is usually the biggest problem. If you are certified, clients expect that you will know more. We'll show you how you use the "tools of the trade" to resolve many of your customers' problems. We've included many of the tips we learned when we started out as WordPerfect certified professionals.

Chapter summary

Chapter 1

In order to help you reach this decision on whether to certify, this chapter is an overview of WordPerfect Corporation, its software products, and its certification programs. WordPerfect has defined several different certification categories. We will discuss the WordPerfect strategy and the role that certification plays in WordPerfect Corporation's overall marketing and support plan. We will try to illustrate why WordPerfect needs people to become certified.

Chapter 2

This chapter details each of the products and the levels at which a person can become certified. We explain the intended audience for each program and the requirements. This section will help you build a certification checklist.

Chapter 3

In order to give you a better idea about how people use certification, we have profiled several WordPerfect certified professionals. Not everyone does what they do; their stories are intended to show you what some people do with the certification.

Chapter 4

This chapter examines the certification test and describes how the tests are developed. We cannot publish actual test questions, but we do discuss the topics. Then we tell you about the process that WordPerfect uses to create test questions. Our goal is to help you determine what to study.

We've included some simple practice questions in chapter 4 so that you can make up your own questions. These practice questions are not intended to actually show you what is on the test or to tell you when you're ready to take the test. Since the tests will change over time, there's no way we can do that. We try to show you how the questions were developed so that you can try to anticipate the types of questions that you might see on a certification exam.

Chapter 5

When you understand the certification process and have decided to pursue it, this chapter will help you prepare for the certification test. We've also included information about self-study (courseware) and classroom courses that can help you prepare for the test by improving your WordPerfect skills.

Chapter 6

When you are ready to take the exam, we talk you through the process of registration. We discuss who to call and what information is required to register. Not everyone is able to pass on the first try; therefore, we offer some ideas about what to do in case of failure.

Chapter 7

The best tips for you to make the most of your certification, which are contained in this chapter, are based upon our correspondence and discussions with other certified professionals and our perspectives.

Chapter 8

An important part of certification is keeping current to ensure that you are relating the absolute latest information to your clients. Your efforts will require the latest information to make decisions about your business. To help with this, we've dedicated an entire chapter to technical support.

Chapter 9

This concluding chapter provides follow-on information to maintain and enhance certification.

Part 1

Certification overview

1

WordPerfect corporate background and certification overview

CHAPTER 1

WordPerfect Corporation was founded in 1979 with a total of two employees and a very simple mission. Founders Alan Ashton and Bruce Bastion wanted to create and sell the best word processing software. They wanted to achieve the goal by marketing software programs that were fully designed, developed, and manufactured in-house.

WordPerfect Corporation's headquarters are located in Orem, Utah, approximately 45 minutes driving time from Salt Lake City. This same area is also the home of the prestigious Brigham Young University and Novell, Inc., which is the maker of popular local area networking software.

WordPerfect Corporation has always prided itself on the unparalleled level of support that the company provides to customers. WordPerfect customer support was for many years free of charge to all registered users of the product. In early 1994, WordPerfect Corporation announced and implemented a pay-for-support program. Under the new policy, customers are entitled to free support within the first 180 days after purchase. Customers pay for support calls after that period. A variety of support contracts are available for corporate clients.

Largely due to this strategy, WordPerfect Corporation's WordPerfect word processing program has dominated the market as the best-selling word processing program on the PC market for several years. WordPerfect Corporation's future plans to succeed in other computer application areas are detailed in its WISE strategy.

⇨ WordPerfect WISE strategy

Various computer companies in the early 1990s developed applications that work together to help a user more efficiently accomplish a task. An example of this would be Microsoft Windows, a PC environment that supports a graphics user interface. In 1993, WordPerfect Corporation announced the WordPerfect Information Systems Environment (WISE) strategy. WISE is the WordPerfect

Corporation strategy for integrating a series of products to help a user perform his or her job.

The WordPerfect WISE strategy ties together four major elements of working with PC-based computer programs:

- Information processing
- Information sharing
- Information presentation
- Information distributing

Information processing addresses the fact that information gets into a computer environment through some form of data entry, such as a word processor, a spreadsheet, or a database. This portion of the strategy seeks to link the *ways* that users create data, which creates a common user interface.

When information is available electronically, it is shared. *Information sharing* addresses the means by which we share information electronically via existing electronic mail systems and also through new and undefined systems that will be designed to better meet user needs and requirements.

Information presentation deals with the graphical representation of data that is stored on computers. Literally, a picture is worth a thousand words. Graphical representations of data make it easier to understand complex and abstract relationships that can only be recognized by reviewing large quantities of raw data.

Information distributing is the bridge that allows for that processing, sharing, and presenting of data in the WISE strategy to be joined. Distributing allows for file compatibility amongst the software products and allows you to access files between applications on different platforms, including networks.

WordPerfect's certification programs are closely tied to the WISE strategy and the company's products. Most people are familiar with WordPerfect, the popular word processing program that is the cornerstone of the company's product line. WordPerfect is available

for a variety of different computer operating systems including DOS, Windows, Macintosh, and Unix.

The original WordPerfect program did everything an electronic typewriter would do. These functions included text entry, formatting, and printing. That same computer that ran WordPerfect could use other programs to perform other tasks, such as calculating tabular data (spreadsheets) or organizing related groups of information (databases).

Today's WordPerfect is more than the original in that it has grown to include additional functions. The program is perhaps best known for its desktop publishing (DTP) capabilities. DTP allows the creator of a document to have greater control over the appearance of the document and placement of words and graphics on the page.

WordPerfect also includes an extensive dictionary, thesaurus, and grammar checking capability. (WordPerfect Corporation acquired and integrated the popular Grammatik grammar checking software.) The 6.0 version of WordPerfect includes the ability to create links from one point in a document to another point in that document or even to another document; the linking capability is called *Hypertext*. Other features of 6.0 include embedding sound or video clips in a document and facsimile capabilities.

WordPerfect for Windows features all of the WordPerfect for DOS features and additional features that are incorporated into the Microsoft Windows environment.

WordPerfect Office has been commercially available for several years. This product has never been actively advertised in the media the way the word processing program has been marketed. Starting as a menu-oriented electronic mail system for local area networks, WordPerfect Office (now called Novell GroupWise) has grown to become a multifaceted Windows-based application: electronic mail, project management, calendaring, and scheduler.

WordPerfect Office/Novell GroupWise is important in that it introduces users to a new environment, the computer network. More than just electronic mail, Office allows users to create and maintain

an electronic calendar of their activities. Users can choose to share that calendar with others or hide the details of the schedule and let others know when they are busy.

WordPerfect InForms takes the idea of a paper-based form and makes the form electronic. The application allows users to create a form, fill in the various fields with data, and then define how the data should be stored. Coupled with this ability to gather and store information is the capability to write to a variety of third-party database products, or send the information to another computer over a network.

InForms is a *mail-enabled* application, meaning that it uses the electronic mail capabilities of WordPerfect Office/Novell GroupWise to move completed forms around the network. The InForms program also has the capability of creating, managing, and recognizing electronic signatures that allow computer forms to be "signed" as if paper documents.

The WordPerfect Certified Perfect Partner program

The WordPerfect Certified Perfect Partner program was created to organize the WordPerfect Corporate marketing and support channel. Perfect Partners range from large reseller organizations and support companies to individual consultants that support a single product. WordPerfect Corporation's certifications program members can be part of the Perfect Partner program.

Throughout the book, "certified partners" are people who are certified on particular products at different levels of certification.

WordPerfect Corporation structured its certification program differently than any other software manufacturer. Besides recognizing software support professionals, the WordPerfect program recognizes users who demonstrate expertise in using a particular product.

WordPerfect certification defines four separate layers that target different groups of people who work in different portions of the computer industry:

- ➢ Business credential
- ➢ Professional credential
- ➢ System Engineer credential
- ➢ Certified instructor

The *Certified Business Credential* (CBC) has been defined to recognize users who are expert at using WordPerfect Corporation's products to solve common business problems. At this time, the CBC credential is available for WordPerfect for DOS or Windows.

The *Certified Professional Credential* (CPC) is targeted at support personnel in both networked and stand-alone environments. A CPC credential is available for WordPerfect InForms and WordPerfect word processing (WordPerfect for DOS or Windows).

The *Certified Systems Engineer* (CSE) credential is available to people who install, configure, and maintain WordPerfect's networked products. A CSE credential is available for WordPerfect Office and InForms products. An *Enterprise Certified System Engineer* (ECSE) credential is available for those who have experience installing, using, and troubleshooting the network products (InForms and Office).

The *Certified Instructor* title is awarded to individuals who have achieved either a Certified Systems Engineer (CSE) or Certified Professional Credential (CPC) and demonstrated the ability to train. Training ability can be demonstrated by submitting a demo tape of the candidate teaching a portion of a course selected by WordPerfect certification, or by holding another recognized credential. WordPerfect will grant instructor status to state-certified teachers and Novell Certified NetWare instructors, Lotus Certified Notes instructors, and other programs that will be considered on an individual basis.

The benefits at each level of certification vary and are dependent upon the level of certification you acquire. At the highest level of

certification, the Enterprise Certified System Engineer can expect to receive technical and marketing support from WordPerfect Corporation. (Chapter 2 details exactly what the benefits are, but broadly defined they include a special-support telephone line and information about leads generated by WordPerfect Corporation advertising and sales staffs.)

All certifications can be achieved after passing a rigorous computer-based exam. This test can be taken at either Drake or Sylvan testing centers worldwide. *The actual test questions and the determination of passing are developed by WordPerfect Corporation.* The independent testing centers ensure that the tests are delivered fairly; a center is typically located in a candidate's local area.

Courses that can prepare you for the certification exam are available from any WordPerfect Authorized Training Center (ATC) or Authorized Training Associate (ATA). WordPerfect ATCs are commercial training organizations that maintain a staff of WordPerfect-Certified Instructors. Classes are usually conducted over 2–3 full days, although some centers may choose to offer several week-long night programs.

You can also become certified by successfully completing a WordPerfect training course led by a Certified Instructor and conducted by a WordPerfect ATA. An ATA might be an educational institution or training organization that is usually nonprofit, or an ATA might be a company's internal employee training department with a Certified Instructor on staff.

You now have an understanding of what WordPerfect Corporation is about and the products they have created. You can see how their programs are interconnected through the WISE strategy and how closely this parallels their certification program. Further chapters provide greater detail regarding the different certification program levels.

WordPerfect certification programs

CHAPTER 2

This chapter examines each of the WordPerfect certification options in detail. We will talk about the target audience for each certification title, what the specific requirements for certification are, and the benefits. We've developed checklists that you can use to compare and evaluate your certification and preparation choices.

Certifications available include:

- ➢ Certified Instructor (CI)
- ➢ Enterprise Certified System Engineer (ECSE)
- ➢ Certified System Engineer (CSE)
- ➢ Certified Professional Credential (CPC)
- ➢ Certified Business Credential (CBC)

It is important to note that there are actually 13 different types of certification discussed in this chapter (see chart). The Certified Instructor credential is available for each of the four products covered by the program. Certified System Engineer is only available for InForms and Office. Certified professional is available for WordPerfect for DOS or Windows, and for InForms. Certified Business Credential is only available for WordPerfect for DOS or Windows.

Certification examinations	WordPerfect Windows	WordPerfect DOS	InForms	WordPerfect Office/Novell GroupWise
CI	■	■	■	■
ECSE				■
CSE			■	■
CPC	■	■	■	■
CBC	■	■		

Shading indicates level of certification available for each product.

A WordPerfect Essential Skills training kit is available to help students in their preparation for all of the WordPerfect word processing certification courses. The essential skills kit concentrates on fundamental word processing skills and keyboarding proficiency.

Certification candidates can prepare for each of the exams by taking a course from a WordPerfect authorized training associate (ATA) or authorized training center (ATC) or through self-study. ATA and ATC requirements were discussed in chapter 1. Courseware (self-study) kits can be purchased directly from WordPerfect or ATCs. To find the ATC closest to you, contact WordPerfect Corporation's certification department at 1-800-993-3700.

The difference between ATC and ATA to the student is that the training course at the ATA ends with an instructor assessment of the candidate's skills. This assessment takes into account all the work that the student has performed in the course, as well as the score on an instructor-administered exam. The ATA option places the final decision for awarding an on-site credential in the hands of a Certified Instructor. For this reason the ATA course of study is usually spread over an entire school semester, as many as 16 weeks, or possibly longer.

While the ATA preparation program includes a lot of hands-on classroom work, almost all students will have to spend additional time studying and reviewing during the course and afterward prior to taking the examination. If the student doesn't have access to a computer at home or at the workplace, he or she should ask about available classroom time or lab time for access to a computer for study and review.

Candidates preparing at an ATC complete a shorter course of study. The duration of a WordPerfect certification preparation course at a training center can be 2–3 days in duration depending on the product (WordPerfect, Office, or InForms). While the course of study at the ATC is shorter, it is also generally assumed that the student is going to go home or to his or her office and study after completing the class.

Candidates choosing to take a course at an ATC, ATA, or preparing through self-study must successfully pass the certification exam at a testing center before a WordPerfect certification credential is awarded.

Courseware

WordPerfect courseware provides material and lessons that allow you to simulate an office environment and practice tasks that are performed in business.

Courseware packages that are available:

- WordPerfect 6.0 DOS Professional Skills Study Kit
- WordPerfect 6.0 DOS Business Skills Study Kit
- WordPerfect 6.0 DOS Essential Skills Study Kit
- WordPerfect 6.0 Windows Professional Skills Study Kit
- WordPerfect 6.0 Windows Business Skills Study Kit
- WordPerfect Office/Novell GroupWise 4.0 System Engineer Skills
- WordPerfect InForms 1.0 System Engineer Skills *(Includes Designer Skills Study Kit)
- WordPerfect InForms 1.0 Form Designer Skills Study Kit

Candidates should be aware that WordPerfect has developed a series of "transitional" courseware packages to make it easier to learn WordPerfect by using examples from another software package that they might know.

Some certification candidates may choose to develop their own form of study (see chapter 5) or purchase a commercially available courseware kit from a source other than WordPerfect Corporation. We should warn you that the WordPerfect certification exams are performance based. Performance-based testing, defined very simply, means that if you have not performed these specific tasks, you will probably be unable to pass the exam.

Many people do not pass the exam on the first attempt; fortunately, there is no limit on the number of times that you can take any particular certification exam imposed by WordPerfect Corporation.

Each certification granted is unique and different from all others. It is possible for someone who has passed the certification exam on InForms to state that he or she are WordPerfect certified, but in the eyes of WordPerfect Corporation, that person is certified on InForms only. We suggest that if you plan on working with several products, you should pursue several different certifications.

As a general rule, all certified partners must recertify within 6 months of the release of a major new version of the product for which they are certified, or whenever notified by the WordPerfect Corporation Certification Department.

When you are certified, you will qualify to receive special benefits from WordPerfect depending on the level and program you choose to certify on. There are three levels of benefits:

- Standard benefits available for all the levels of certification.
- Membership benefits available for ECSE, CSE, CIs, ATC, and ATA programs.
- Strategic partner benefits are available for those individuals or organizations that WordPerfect evaluates and are found to meet specific criteria. Strategic partner benefits are available for ECSE, CSE, CI, ATC, and ATA.

You can learn more about any of these programs by contacting WordPerfect Corporation's Certification department at 1-800-993-3700. When inquiring about the availability and location of certification courses, be specific about which course you want to take. Not all training associates or centers are certified on all products. If you plan on taking more than one class at a center, inquire about multiple-class discounts.

Essential skills credential

The essential skills credential has been defined to recognize users who are qualified at using WordPerfect Corporation's word processing products to solve common business problems in an office environment. It represents the essential word processing skills that every computer user should be able to perform.

Certified Business Credential

What is CBC?

The Certified Business Credential (CBC) has been defined to recognize users who are expert at using WordPerfect Corporation's word processing products to solve common business problems in an office environment. It represents the word processing skills that more experienced computer users, sometimes referred to as "power users," should be able to perform. At this time, the CBC credential is available for WordPerfect for DOS or Windows version 6.0.

Who is a good candidate for the CBC program?

A person who uses WordPerfect daily to either automate his or her normal job tasks or assist others in the use of the WordPerfect product's operation. Someone who feels he or she has a good understanding of the product, a true end-user, such as an administrative assistant, secretary, or other support staff who utilize the product.

The Certified Business Credential would be especially useful for someone returning to the work force after several years absence. With this certification, a job candidate can determine how well he or she knows the WordPerfect product and prove to the prospective employer their competency level.

College or high school students who have just completed courses in WordPerfect at the different levels could qualify and pass the exam. This is especially valuable to students at schools participating in the ATA program.

 Prerequisites

There are no stated WordPerfect certification prerequisites for the CBC program. Knowledge of DOS and the basic operations of a personal computer are assumed. If pursuing certification for WordPerfect for Windows, a thorough knowledge of the Windows environment, in addition to DOS, is assumed. No knowledge of computer hardware is required.

Knowledge of common office skills and procedures is very helpful but not required. It is often difficult to understand complicated functions of features such as a mail merge if you've never performed this activity or if you won't be using mail merge. Experience with all the tools that a program has to automate an office will be the key to understanding office functions and ultimately using the program to its maximum potential.

 Preparation

The CBC exam is based on the student's ability to complete certain predefined job tasks and demonstrate job skills. The courseware and the ATA or ATC classroom course are structured to present each one of the job tasks that a student must be able to complete. The student should plan on spending extra time prior to an exam to review all functions and features that are not used on a regular basis.

A WordPerfect kit for essential skills is available to help the student prepare.

Job tasks that are evaluated include:

- Installing the WordPerfect program
- Customizing the WordPerfect environment
- Managing files

Skills that are evaluated include the ability to use the features of the product to:

- Create a form
- Produce a business letter and envelope
- Create a memo
- Create a resume
- Produce meeting minutes
- Create an agenda
- Design a brochure
- Create a financial statement
- Design a newsletter
- Produce a report

Table 2-1 **List of Available Resources for Preparation for CBC**

	Self-study	Training associate	Training center
Student kit	WPCorp or other	WPCorp or other	WPCorp
Take course		X	X
Study time	Highest	Lowest	Medium
Assessment	Online practice test	End of course (On-site credential)	Training center test
Exam	X		X

In this chart, "Student Kit" refers to whatever source the student used for training. Candidates choosing self-study or a formal course with a training associate (ATA) would use materials that were either developed by WordPerfect Corporation (WPCorp), or purchased or developed by an instructor. The "Take Course" field signifies that candidates who choose to prepare at either a training associate and training center need to complete a course. "Study Time" is our estimate of the relative amount of time required outside of the

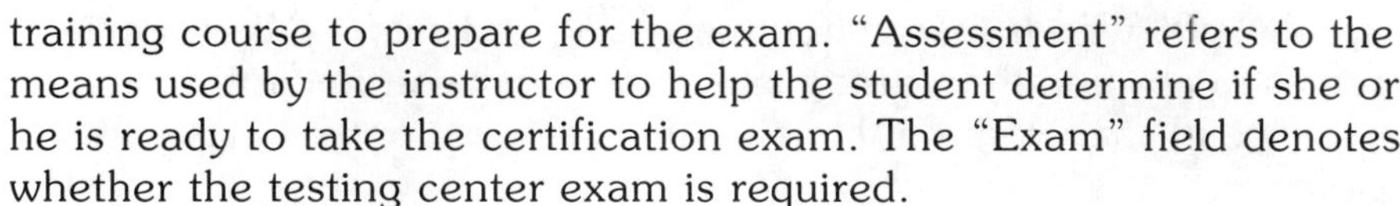

training course to prepare for the exam. "Assessment" refers to the means used by the instructor to help the student determine if she or he is ready to take the certification exam. The "Exam" field denotes whether the testing center exam is required.

Benefits

The standard benefits at the CBC level include:

- Certificate
- Membership card
- Subscription to the certification newsletter
- WordPerfect promotional gift package

Certified Professional Credential

What is a CPC?

The Certified Professional Credential (CPC) is targeted at the user who is technically inclined to deal with advanced features of the programs. You can approach this certification from three different angles because you have a choice of software packages to test on. A CPC is available for WordPerfect Office, InForms, and WordPerfect word processing (WordPerfect for DOS or Windows version 6.0). This certification serves as a prerequisite to becoming a CI.

Who is a good candidate for the CPC program?

The individual who is in a software-support role, a trainer, a consultant, or a reseller of WordPerfect products is a good CPC candidate. This person has mastered and demonstrated troubleshooting expertise at the desktop level.

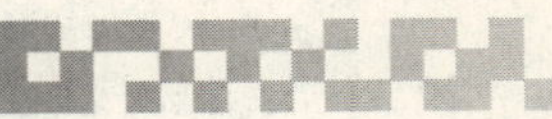

The individual who is involved in marketing and sales of WordPerfect products might find it advantageous to also have an in-depth knowledge of the program. Holding this certification will prove that knowledge.

Another good candidate for CPC might be the person who has chosen to specialize in one vertical solution with the WordPerfect program, like legal functions. This will not only give you credibility on the vertical solution you specialize in, but also the overall product knowledge.

Prerequisites

You can think of the CPC as one step past the CBC program. Although CBC is not a prerequisite, you must have an understanding of the basics, along with the administrative skills that surpass the CBC level to be comfortable with this level. You must have knowledge of products in stand-alone and networked environments.

Preparation

The CPC level lets you test your knowledge on WordPerfect Office, InForms, or WordPerfect DOS/Windows.

For Office, you must be able to plan, create and troubleshoot the following:

- Preference setups
- Add and delete users
- Single post office installation
- Advanced feature set (i.e., rules, routing, proxy, etc.)
- Maintenance options

For InForms, you must be able to plan, create, and troubleshoot the following:

- Form layout
- Database linking
- Calculations
- Form distribution and query

For WordPerfect DOS and Windows you must possess troubleshooting skills on the following:

- Setting up WordPerfect
- Managing files
- Formatting documents
- Editing documents
- Automating tasks
- Working with professional publications
- Working with special features
- Printing

List of Available Resources for Preparation for CPC Table 2-2

	Self-study	**Training associate**	**Training center**
Student kit	WPCorp or other	WPCorp or other	WPCorp
Take course		X	X
Study time	Highest	Lowest	Medium
Assessment	Online practice test	End of course (On-site credential)	Training center test
Exam	X		X

Benefits

The standard benefits at the CPC level include:

- Certificate
- Membership card
- Subscription to the certification newsletter
- WordPerfect promotional gift package

Certified Systems Engineer

What is CSE?

The enterprise CSE (ECSE) and the Certified Systems Engineer (CSE) credentials are available to system integrators and administrators of WordPerfect's networked products. This program is a little different than the CBC and CPC programs in that it allows your emphases to be focused on a larger environment in which you must have network experience.

You'll also see that this program doesn't require that you be an expert in word processing. Your knowledge needs to be focused on setting up and installing the products in network environments, although you must still have adequate product-use skills within the desktop environment. The CSE credential is available for WordPerfect Office and InForms products.

WordPerfect product reseller organizations and training organizations that are members of the Certified Perfect Partner Program are required to have CSEs. This program also serves as a prerequisite for CPP and CI.

Who is a good candidate for the CSE program?

Someone who is currently a Novell CNE or CNI would have the network experience required. Others are software engineers, computer operators, and technicians who have an understanding of network software maintenance and integration requirements.

WordPerfect Office/Novell GroupWise Certified System Engineer

Knowledge of troubleshooting, maintenance, and error messages for a single host through a local area network (LAN) is essential to become an Office/GroupWise CSE. It is assumed that the Office/GroupWise CSE is able to deal with the following:

- ➢ Asynchronous gateways
- ➢ Remote office
- ➢ Generic gateways
- ➢ Multiple systems merge/release
- ➢ Multiple systems
- ➢ Multiple-domain systems
- ➢ Single-domain systems
- ➢ 3.1 to 4.1 Office system conversion

WordPerfect InForms Certified System Engineer

The InForms CSE test is not related to application features needed by end-users; rather the test is related to skills that are necessary to plan, install, maintain, and troubleshoot within a network environment. Skill level includes the following:

- ➢ System administration
    - Security
    - Network system
    - Stand-alone machine

- ➢ Creation, distribution, and use of forms
  - Query and report
  - Distribution
  - Calculations
  - Links
  - Form layout

Table 2-3 **List of Available Resources for Preparation for CSE**

	Self-study	**Training associate**	**Training center**
Student kit	WPCorp or other	N/A	WPCorp
Take course		N/A	X
Study time	X	N/A	X
Assessment	Online practice test	N/A	Training center test
Exam	X		X

Benefits

The standard benefits at the CSE level include:

- ➢ Certificate
- ➢ Membership card
- ➢ Subscription to the certification newsletter
- ➢ WordPerfect promotional gift package

The membership benefits include:

- ➢ Membership gift package
- ➢ Product specific periodicals
- ➢ Logo for advertising
- ➢ Discount on permanent evaluation software
- ➢ Discount on certification exams

- Discount on customer support Folio INFOBASE (described in chapter 7)
- Can qualify for Certified Perfect Partner Program (CPP)
- Priority phone support

Certified Instructor

What is CI?

The Certified Instructor title is awarded to individuals who have achieved either ECSE, CSE, or CPC and demonstrated the ability to train.

Who is a good candidate for the CI program?

Consultants, WordPerfect Office/Novell GroupWise trainers, community education instructors, professors, and teachers are good candidates for this program. Not only do you have to have a good understanding of the software at all levels, but you should have the patience and personality it takes to teach others software products.

Prerequisites

All Certified Instructor candidates must first demonstrate product knowledge by passing the CSE or CPC requirements and meeting the following requirements:

- Have 6 months or more classroom training experience
- Training on at least one WordPerfect product
- Provide hands-on training with supporting student materials
- Show proof of adequate software licensing
- Provide regular reporting about WordPerfect training

The process of becoming a CI involves a little more work than just passing either the CSE or CPC exams. You must apply to the program by requesting from WordPerfect an electronic application that is provided on disk. You should request this disk about the same time that you are preparing for the exam; then, when you pass the exam, you will be ready to apply for the CI status.

Checklist for electronic WordPerfect application for Certified Instructor

You will need the following information at hand when you begin to fill out the application disk. You will have a choice of menu options. All options must be completed before being submitted.

Menu option 1—Main entry

- Name:
- Social security number:
- Company address:
- Mailing address:
- Telephone:
- Self-employed (Y/N) and hours per week:
- In-house trainer (Y/N) and hours per week:
- Trainer at commercial training center (Y/N) and hours per week:
- Educator (Y/N) and hours per week:

(Hours per week represent the time that you spend training in the selected training environment. Educator refers to a teacher at a school or university.)

Menu option 2—Additional information

- Exams passed (WordPerfect 6.0 Professional, InForms Professional, WordPerfect Office/Novell GroupWise 4.0 CSE, InForms 1.0 CSE):

- Other certificates (certified NetWare instructor, current teaching certificate):
- Product licenses:
- Reason for applying for the Certified Instructor status:

(Make sure you include all tests you passed because this will give you more referrals and more support benefits. You should write one or two paragraphs about your reasons for applying for certification.)

Menu option 3—Business information

- Average pricing:
  - Training:
  - Consulting:
- Percent of revenue from:
  - Training:
  - Consulting:
  - Training materials:
- Refund/satisfaction guarantee:
- Cancellation policy:
- Minimum enrollment policy:

(Fees from instructor to instructor will vary depending on market or geographic location of your training. All these numbers can be estimated. You should be aware of the WordPerfect satisfaction guarantee that requires instructors to return the class fee, less the price of student materials, if the student is not satisfied.)

Menu option 4—Business information (continued)

- Do you provide after-training telephone support? (Y/N)
- Do you send newsletters to clients featuring WordPerfect product information? If so, how often is it distributed?
- Have you contacted the WordPerfect area manager?
- Have you attended WordPerfect Corporation conferences during last year?

- ➢ Association memberships:
- ➢ Additional involvement:

(Association memberships could include: ACTS (Ziff Institute), Help Desk Institute, NATD, ICTA, CNEPA, and ATEC. Additional involvement could include any other computer-related activity, published teaching materials, articles, books, starting local user groups, or organizing WordPerfect support channels.

Menu option 5—Training information

- ➢ How long in training business (in years):
- ➢ How long training WordPerfect products:
- ➢ Geographic scope of training (local, national, regional, international):
- ➢ Average training hours per week:
- ➢ Percent of training for WordPerfect products:
- ➢ Average number of students per month trained on WordPerfect products:
- ➢ Average number of students per class:
- ➢ Do you use classroom assistants? (Y/N) (Note: Classroom assistants do not have to be WordPerfect certified.)

Menu option 6—Training information (continued)

- ➢ Methods of assessing skill levels before and after class:
- ➢ Training philosophy:

(While not required, it is appropriate for instructors to create a short survey that students would complete after finishing a class to gauge their satisfaction. The training philosophy of most instructors is based upon the adult education paradigm, which states that both the instructor and the student are jointly responsible for creating a positive learning environment.)

Menu option 7—Course offerings

- ➢ WordPerfect
- ➢ WordPerfect Office/Novell GroupWise
- ➢ InForms
- ➢ Presentations
- ➢ DataPerfect
- ➢ WordPerfect Works

(Notes: Make sure that you list all the different versions and platforms training on. You should have training materials prepared, or be aware of a source from which you could purchase materials, for all products you select.)

Menu option 8—Referral directory information

- ➢ Do you wish to receive client referrals from WordPerfect? (Y/N)
- ➢ Please provide name, city, state, and phone number to go into directory listing:

(Notes: List the closest large city or metropolitan area. It is to your advantage to answer "Yes" to receive client referrals from WordPerfect if you plan on marketing your training on WordPerfect products. If you're out there and you are qualified WordPerfect wants to refer you.)

Menu option 9—Specializations

(Specify only one specialization in each category.)

- ➢ **Service**
  - Training
  - Consulting
  - Installation
  - System integration
  - Macro programming
  - Courseware development
  - Support
  - Other

➢ **Vertical market**
  - Legal
  - Banking
  - Corporate
  - Publishing
  - Medical
  - Government
  - Education
  - Other

(If you specialized, you have to select one choice from Service and Vertical Market categories. It is important to answer this correctly so that you will be matched up with clients that seek your specialization. Most instructors base their particular area of specialization on a field they previously worked in.)

Menu option 10—Final checklist

➢ 20- to 30-minute amateur videotape teaching a topic from a list of choices supplied by WordPerfect.

➢ Copy of Novell Certified NetWare Instructor certificate.

➢ Copy of current teaching certificate with a business education specialization.

➢ Résumé.

➢ Nonrefundable fee.

➢ Sample courseware (couple of pages).

➢ Brochure.

(Notes: Make backups of the application disk and duplicate all materials before sending everything to WordPerfect. Send current courseware, which might include booklets, handouts, or disks. You could also state here that you use a particular training company's materials. An application fee is also required at the time you submit the application; the fee was $200 in mid-1994.)

Teaching ability

You have to be able to teach to become a CI. Training ability can be demonstrated by presenting for review a recognized teaching credential (perhaps a college education degree) or submitting a demo tape of yourself teaching a portion of a course selected by WordPerfect certification. WordPerfect will grant instructor status to state-certified teachers and Novell Certified NetWare Instructors (CNI). A CI is an invaluable asset to an ATA or ATC.

WordPerfect Corporation will contact references and ask about your training skills. Adult education and community education is a good place to start when selecting your references. Realize that you will not be certified if there are any negative reviews from references. If you provide a single false reference, then you can be disqualified.

Benefits

The standard benefits at the CI level include:

- Certificate
- Membership card
- Subscription to the certification newsletter

The membership benefits include:

- Membership gift package
- Product-specific periodicals
- Logo for advertising
- Discount on permanent evaluation software
- Discount on certification exams
- Discount on customer support Folio INFOBASE
- Instructor kits
- Study kits
- Listing in the *WordPerfect Certified Training Directory*

The strategic partner benefits include:

- Prerelease software (product-specific)
- Free access to customer support's Folio INFOBASE
- 50 percent off one conference hosted by WordPerfect Corporation
- Invitations to local events sponsored by WordPerfect

Certification profiles

CHAPTER 3

An important way of learning about something new is through the experiences of others. Perhaps you know someone who decided to try something that you were interested in, and he or she subsequently told you that it was fun and really was not as difficult or dangerous as presumed. If the person were a friend who you knew fairly well, you might try it. This chapter introduces you to some new friends.

You will meet a group of people who have taken the time to pursue and successfully obtain WordPerfect certification. Upon reading the stories, you will find that their success came as the result of much hard work.

The profiles were derived from surveys and interviews with people who were certified under the WordPerfect 5.1, WordPerfect 6.0, and Office CSE programs. Sometimes in their words, this chapter will show you how being certified has helped enhance their business skills and experiences.

⇨ Carolyn Woodie

Carolyn Woodie started her computer consulting business, which specializes in small office automation, in 1984. She began her business career, after raising a family, as a administrative assistant working in a computerized office environment.

Office automation is a specialty that many WordPerfect-certified partners are involved in. Office automation specialists generally help office workers accomplish their traditional jobs using new technology. This involves bringing new products into the office, setting them up, instructing the staff on proper use, and then helping customize the products to the office staff's particular needs.

Carolyn found learning about computers and software interesting. Several associates commented that she seemed to master new software packages quickly with relative ease. In 1986, after finding it impossible to keep up with using several different word processing packages and subsequent software upgrades, she began to specialize

in teaching WordPerfect word processing classes. Carolyn tested and became certified by WordPerfect Corporation in 1989 on WordPerfect 5.0.

Carolyn says, "Just preparing for and taking the various certification tests has required that I really delve deeply into the more obscure features of the products." She feels today that she is a better instructor and consultant because she really knows the capabilities of the software and is fully prepared to meet client needs.

Carolyn, as many Certified Instructors reported, has confidence in the WordPerfect Certification Program. It is great to be able to recommend other Certified Instructors to her clients for work in branch offices located in other parts of the country.

As a WordPerfect Certified Instructor, Carolyn is busy. She was the cofounder of the Baltimore WordPerfect Users Group. Her client database includes universities, government agencies, and small businesses. When she is not training, Carolyn regularly speaks at conferences and conventions about WordPerfect applications and the use of computerized technology in the modern office.

It's hard for Carolyn to imagine being a Certified Instructor and not attending at least a few of the WordPerfect conferences. (WordPerfect's conferences are discussed in more detail in chapter 7.) A conference is an opportunity for hands-on training on the new products. She stated that this is a "must" to keep up with the latest WordPerfect products.

"Networking with other Certified Instructors who do what I do around the country is invaluable. We discuss teaching techniques, marketing strategies, and training problems. I have developed a support group around the country and have continued relationships with some of the Certified Instructors over years," Carolyn said.

In any industry, it is necessary to keep up your education or you will become complacent in what you do. You will not remain sharp and challenged. "As a Certified Instructor, the conferences provide a place to be recharged. I return with more training ideas and methods, a greater knowledge of the software," she said.

During the course of your training career, every computer instructor runs into the student who has had a bad training experience with an instructor who had poor training qualifications. In many cases, a bad training experience can be very costly, not to mention all the wasted time. In most cases, inadequate training will discourage a student from using the software package and, in some cases, discourage the use of computers in general.

Although not every client you will train will be knowledgeable about the certification program or the requirements you had to meet, Carolyn believes that after a good training experience with a Certified Instructor her clients are convinced about the benefits of certification and her credentials.

Lisa Sarubbi

Lisa Sarubbi, the founder of Data Works, Inc., became certified in January 1992. "The original reason I became certified was for the credibility factor I believed it would give to clients," she recalls. "Being an independent contractor makes it that much harder to sell yourself. I believed the certification would give me the edge I needed over other contractors and companies."

Lisa found that the greatest benefit to being certified is networking with other certified people. The certified people she has met have led to many new and exciting opportunities. Most of Lisa's clientele come from referrals that she receives from other Certified Instructors.

Lisa has found going to the WordPerfect Conferences very beneficial (chapter 7). After attending one of the conferences, Lisa was so inspired and motivated by the other conference attendees that she promptly became certified at the next higher level of certification that WordPerfect offered at the time.

Lisa, along with other certified people in her geographical area, was involved in setting up a WordPerfect workshop in Annapolis, Maryland. The purpose of the workshop was to assemble a group of Certified Instructors who were interested in training on the new release of WordPerfect 6.0. The instructors who led the workshop were WordPerfect Corporation employees. All the people who attended this workshop were there for the same reason: to prepare for the upcoming certification tests.

Meeting new people has opened the door to new opportunities. Lisa's business has placed emphasis on WordPerfect macro programming, where she writes "suites" of macros to automate the modern office. One of her largest clients is the United States Department of Justice. She also writes the user guides and documentation to go along with her customized macros.

When not doing macro programming for companies, government agencies, and small businesses, she is training and performing technical support for her clients.

Lisa feels certification bolstered her credibility with clientele because many of the people she trains are either support analysts or people who are already proficient in WordPerfect. When she is conducting end-user training, her clients like to tell the employees that "We hired a WordPerfect Certified Instructor."

Due to the in-depth knowledge of WordPerfect that Lisa has acquired, she was contacted by a publisher to write a book about WordPerfect for Windows. Her book is used in many colleges throughout the United States. She believes that her WordPerfect certification gave validity to her knowledge of the subject.

Debbie Chelius

"My job responsibilities steered me into getting WordPerfect-certified," says Debbie, who became certified in 1991. "I work for a school district (and I am) in charge of computer operations and technical support of many software packages. WordPerfect was one of the packages I was supporting," she said. Many people have become certified for the same reason.

"After learning all the different features and showing the other users all the interesting things the program could do, I became involved in teaching in the community adult-education programs for local school districts," Debbie said. Community or adult-education programs provide important and valuable practice for many instructors to build there training skills.

"After automating the offices and doing all the training, I felt I had an in-depth knowledge of the program," she said. After hearing about the WordPerfect certification program, Debbie decided to take the certification test to challenge her knowledge of the program. "Just preparing for the test taught me more about the (application), which I later turned around and taught to others."

When Debbie became certified, more career opportunities opened up. She started her own computer consulting company on a part-time basis. The company consisted primarily of software training, which included writing training materials and documentation. She was contacted by a local training center that was looking for instructors to teach. Debbie got the job over the other applicants because of her certification credential.

Being certified put her on the WordPerfect certification referral list, and she was getting referrals from WordPerfect Corporation. Using the WordPerfect logo in local advertising was a definite advantage because her name stood out over other advertisers. Clients do appreciate the fact that an instructor has gone all out to become proficient with a product and is certified by the software manufacturer.

"Recertification was tough but definitely worth it!" said Debbie. She reports that the process of preparing for the exam has helped expand her knowledge of the 6.0 word processing products. Debbie, already a Certified Instructor, estimated that she dedicated two solid months to mastering the new products to the point where she was comfortable taking the certification exam. "When I first arrived at the testing center, I was very nervous about the computer-based test, but once I started, I found it very fair," Debbie said.

She highly recommends that anyone looking for an edge over the competition should be certified. Although you have to invest time and money to proceed with becoming certified, it will be beneficial to you. In the early days of certification, the program only let you become certified on the WordPerfect word processing package. The new applications add a whole new meaning to certification; you have different choices of software packages to become certified on.

Andrew Caufield

Andrew works for one of the largest resellers of computer hardware and software in his region. He is part of a full-time departmental staff for technical service and support. When he started this job, he spent most of his time configuring and installing PCs at client offices. Having worked for the reseller for almost three years, he has graduated to designing network solutions for customers and troubleshooting problems.

He spends much of his time troubleshooting. "It's tough sometimes because on Sunday you think you know what you'll be doing for the next week, but when you arrive Monday morning a customer will call with a problem, and the next thing I know it's Wednesday," he said.

Andrew commented on a common trend in the service and support industry: "People just don't seem to stay in one place for very long. If you work a particular product real well you either get promoted and make more money or after a while you move on (change jobs)."

Andrew started working with WordPerfect Office 3.0 several years ago. He reported that the customer was loyal to WordPerfect word processing products on stand-alone PCs and decided to purchase Office when they installed a LAN. "Given my working knowledge of WordPerfect, I was impressed with Office because all the WordPerfect keystrokes worked the same way," he said.

Andrew learned about the Office certification program while completing his Novell certified NetWare engineer (CNE) course. "I learned a lot of Novell the hard way by sitting and working with a

Novell LAN," he said. "My employer agreed to pay for some Novell courses at a local training center, and I saw WordPerfect training was offered, as well. I asked the training center about WordPerfect certification, got some basic information, and just decided to challenge the Office test."

His first attempt at the test was a bad one. Andrew didn't take the time to research what was on the exam; he had only taken a look at the manuals during lunch for a few days before the exam. That didn't help much, and he failed. Afterward, he was encouraged because, as he put it, "I failed, but I wasn't blown away. I knew a lot of the material covered on the exam from experience. I called WordPerfect and they said the score was near passing."

Andrew spent much more time preparing the second time around. "I built a small LAN and really starting working with the product," he said. Andrew reported that the information gained from the failed exam actually contributed to his second attempt, which he passed. The second time around he worked with the product several evenings a week over a 5-week period for a total of 24 hours. "I really had to read up about gateways, though! I had no way to create (an internetwork of two or more linked networks) in the lab." He estimates that his total time working with the application and reading was about 40 hours.

We asked Andrew what he thought about the WordPerfect exams using performance-based testing. "This test was totally different than anything I had seen before, and I've taken a bunch of Novell CNE exams. I liked it," he said. "This test asked about how the product really works, rather than asking a question about information taken from a book."

⇨ Overview

What do the certified people have in common? All reported that they were comfortable experimenting with the personal computer and learning about new applications on the PC. Training other clients might not fill their entire day, but they all use the WordPerfect products in their businesses:

- Customizing macros
- Office automation
- Working on setting up local user groups
- Running their own businesses
- Writing books

Although many are certified on WordPerfect products, which accounts for a substantial portion of their business, they also support other software products. We found that most of the other software products complemented the WordPerfect application environments.

Part 2

Examination guidance

What is a certification exam?

CHAPTER 4

All WordPerfect certification exams are "performance-based," meaning that the candidate is expected to have actually performed some of the operations in order to pass the test. We asked Gary Ashton, director of WordPerfect Corporation's certification department, to elaborate: "The test questions challenge your expertise." This chapter is intended to give you some idea about what you can expect from a certification exam.

The most important concept that a certification candidate can understand is how the tests are developed. Understanding how the tests are developed helps greatly in the preparation process and also helps the candidate become a better user of the product.

The process of developing a WordPerfect certification exam begins with the development of a *work model*. The work model is a statement or statements attempting to summarize a user's knowledge that will permit completion of a task. "The ability to install a basic WordPerfect Office system consisting of one post office" might be categorized as a work model. An InForms work model might revolve around "using the product to create an employment application with a corporate logo at the top of the page." A WordPerfect work model might be "to create a large, multichapter document using the Master Document feature."

This process of assessing the skills needed to accomplish a task is also referred to as job analysis and is used to determine the product skills of people who would be considered experts. WordPerfect determines this through interviews with users (inside and outside the company), focus groups (users who are asked to give their opinions about various products and features), and researching questions that have been asked of the product development team.

Three different types of questions can be generated from a work model:

- Conversational
- Procedural
- Causal

Questions that test the candidate's *conversational knowledge* of a product might ask for the definition of a specific product-related term. Given that the candidate is being asked about the installation of a single post-office Office system, the exam might ask, "How many domains need to be defined?" If the candidate understands that the Office domain unit contains post offices, they would be able to answer this question. The answer: "At least one domain needs to be defined to install a single post office system."

A *procedural* question tests the candidate's ability to perform an action that requires a number of steps; the candidate is asked to logically perform an action that has steps. Typical procedural questions ask the applicant to choose which action would come first, or which action should be next. In order to be fair, the test writers try to stay away from factors influenced by the user's style and matters of efficiency (how to do something with the fewest keystrokes).

Using the InForms example of creating an employment application, an example of a procedural question might be, "Identify which of the following steps would be done first: size the field, type the words "First Name" in name box, click on tool palette icon, or choose Position and Size from the Properties menu." Each of these is a step that a candidate would need to perform to define a field. The correct answer: "Click on the tool palette icon first" (then size the field, then enter the field name in the name box, and finally change Position and Size properties of the newly defined field). The candidate would not be able to build the field any other way using these steps.

A *causal* question tests how well a candidate understands the interrelationship of steps in a process. These questions literally "get into your head" to determine how well you know the concept. Causal questions will put forward a procedure or scenario, and ask the candidate to predict what will or should happen next. Often causal questions will describe what happened and ask why.

"Let's take the WordPerfect example to create a large, multichapter document file using the Master Document feature. The master file is titled MASTER.DOC and the subdocuments are SUB1.DOC, SUB2.DOC, and SUB3.DOC. I have expanded the master document and made changes that would affect SUB1.DOC and SUB2.DOC, but

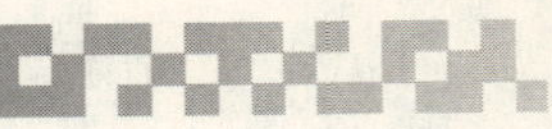

not SUB3.DOC. I select FILE, SAVE, and then EXIT, but later when I look at the subdocument SUB2.DOC, I find that the changes I made to the expanded master have not been reflected in the subdocument. What file contains the changes?"

The correct answer: "The changes were probably saved in the MASTER.DOC file." If the user had chosen to compress the document, he or she would have had the option of selecting whether or not to save each subdocument.

Different questions are important in that one type of question might be inappropriate for testing a candidate's knowledge of a particular feature. By asking a variety of different questions, it becomes easier to accurately test the candidate's actual performance-based expertise.

Each WordPerfect certification exam is taken at a computer, meaning that you will sit at a PC in an authorized testing center and answer questions that are displayed on the PC monitor. You may use either the mouse or the keyboard to answer the questions. The authorized testing centers ensure that there is a degree of security associated with the test. The people working at the testing center make sure candidates don't use prepared notes, collaborate with other people in the room, or leave the testing area with written notes taken during the exam.

Most of the questions are text-based and multiple choice. This means that they are "word" questions; the candidate is asked to read the question and select the best answer from a list of possible answers. Other questions are multi-multiple choice, meaning that there are several possible answers to the question. Multi-multiple choice questions usually appear as a list of answers with the choices "Yes" and "No" next to each answer. After you read the question, you answer "Yes" or "No" as to whether or not this answer is correct. The number of correct answers varies from question to question.

Some of the questions rely on the use of graphics (pictures). When a question involves looking at a graphic, the test system will either display the graphic on the same screen as the question, or you will have to select an option from the screen (usually displayed as a button) that will then display the graphic. Another option or button on the graphic screen will take you back to the exam question text. Some questions call for the candidate to point at a particular spot on the graphic and press the mouse button.

Each certification exam is timed. The amount of time that the candidate will have to complete the exam depends on which test is being taken. The WordPerfect exams are either 1 hour long or 2 hours long depending upon which exam you are taking. When a candidate is taking the exam, the time remaining will be displayed, usually in the upper right-hand corner of the screen. The time to complete the respective tests is as follows:

- ➢ WordPerfect 6.0 DOS Business CBC, 60 minutes
- ➢ WordPerfect 6.0 Windows Business CBC, 60 minutes
- ➢ WordPerfect 6.0 DOS Professional CPC, 120 minutes
- ➢ WordPerfect 6.0 Windows Professional CPC, 120 minutes
- ➢ WordPerfect InForms CPC, 60 minutes
- ➢ WordPerfect InForms CSE, 120 minutes
- ➢ WordPerfect Office CSE, 120 minutes

As we stated in the introduction section, the WordPerfect certification exams are somewhat different than computer-based certification exams offered for other company's certifications. The WordPerfect exams are "performance-based." This means that the candidate who has actually taken the time to use the product and perform each of the operations detailed in the outline of the course will have a definite advantage over someone who has just read the manual.

This is not to say that people who only read and study the product manual and other documentation will not pass. If someone has a background installing, servicing, and using similar products, and she studies the WordPerfect product documentation, she might pass the exam. But again, she has "performed" similar operations and has a background with similar products.

The exams are structured so that someone who didn't know what he was doing would not be able to guess the correct answers.

What kinds of questions are asked?

Note that the question format is usually multiple choice, with some questions having one correct answer and others having multiple correct answers, what WordPerfect refers to as multiple/multiple choice. Many questions are set up by a scenario, a page or two that tells the examinee about a situation, and then a series of subsequent questions is related to that setup. You will not see true-false questions on the exam.

Here is an example of a DOS question that might appear on any WordPerfect product exam that assumes knowledge of DOS. This question was developed by WordPerfect Corporation's Certification Department:

Your computer has 12 MB of RAM. In this sample CONFIG.SYS file, click on the line that instructs the computer to load DOS into the memory block between 1024K and 1088K. (Item Type: Point and Click)

The following information is displayed as a graphic and represents the contents of the PC's CONFIG.SYS file.

```
DEVICE = C:\WINDOWS\HIMEM.SYS
DEVICE = C:\WINDOWS\EMM386.EXE
DOS=HIGH,UMB
FILES=100
BUFFERS=15
SHELL=C:\COMMAND.COM /P/E:512
STACKS=9,256
```

The mouse pointer arrow symbol would be replaced with a cross hair.

This question could be characterized as conversational if it merely asked the user to choose the command that relocates DOS to high memory. Instead, the writer has chosen to ask this as a causal question, requesting a choice regarding which command used resulted in DOS being loaded high. The correct answer is:

`DOS=HIGH, UMB.`

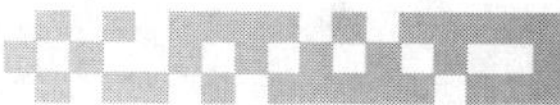

The next sample question was also written by WordPerfect. This question would be appropriate for the Office 4.0 test:

Which of the following considerations will help determine the number of post offices that should be set up in each domain?

A. The number of file servers on the network.

B. The client software which will be used (DOS, Windows, or Macintosh).

C. The anticipated message traffic between users on different file servers.

D. The network software being used and any limitations that the NOS may impose.

If a person were planning on installing a WordPerfect Office 4.0 system, it would be important that she be familiar with the product to the point that she would know the answer to this question.

How would you answer this question? Is choice A correct? Is choice B correct? Is choice C correct? Is choice D correct?

In fact, there are three correct answers to this question: A, C, and D. Before you considered creating post offices, you would need to consider the type of network operating system (answer D), the number of file servers (answer A), and then how much message traffic would travel between users whose accounts are defined on different file servers (C).

The following illustrates the way this same question might be asked on the WordPerfect Office CSE exam:

Which of the following considerations will help determine the number of post offices that should be set up in each domain?

A. YES NO The number of file servers on the network.

B. YES NO The client software which will be used (DOS, Windows, or Macintosh).

C. YES NO The anticipated message traffic between users on different file servers.

D. YES NO The network software being used and any limitations that the NOS may impose.

Notice that you must select either YES or NO in response to each possible answer. The testing system does not suggest how many correct answers there are. Instead, it asks the person taking the test to examine a number of possible choices. The testing system does not allow you to proceed to the next question until after you have chosen a YES or NO response to each answer.

Your weighted score for this question would depend on your response. You do worse if you answer totally incorrectly (as if you had answered that only response C above was correct). If you had selected only one correct answer, you would receive some credit. If you chose two of the four possible correct answers, you'd do better. If you chose all three correct responses, you would receive full credit.

How are the tests and questions developed?

Test questions are developed by a team of technical support professionals and writers who, working with the certification department technical staff, evaluate what skills are important to have regarding the program and determine the best way to test someone's expertise. It is difficult to study for this test by memorizing all the different options of a particular feature; applicants must have used this feature and performed certain crucial tasks.

You will need some experience within a setting that called for the use of this feature in different scenarios in the work environment. That is what makes these tests performance-based. You are being tested on how well you can troubleshoot an example. If you can troubleshoot and figure out what is wrong with a problem or what is missing, it becomes a more accurate way of testing your knowledge about the application.

Many questions do have that close "distracter" answer that is meant to separate the skilled from the book-read only. You should find after taking the practice tests that the answer will become obvious if you truly know your material.

We found many troubleshooting questions that force a candidate to think about *how* or *why* you would need to use a particular feature or perform a particular task. Provided you've done a task, the question asks what happens behind the scenes. Where did you go wrong? The questions make you analyze many different scenarios.

If you are fortunate enough to be in a technical support job for one or more of the products being tested, you will find the test comparable to typical work situations that you have encountered. If you are new to the product, you will really have to practice using all the features and create all types of situations.

What is the scoring system?

The scoring system is a point-based system. The questions are weighted and points are given for correct answer, skipped answer, or incorrect answer. The exact weighting of any particular question is not disclosed by WordPerfect Corporation.

The total passing score was set by an overall average of beta testers for the exams. Beta testers include the corporation's users, outside users, and random candidates. A *cut score* was set from their average; the cut score represents what the people at the WordPerfect Certification Department believe should be the total passing score.

Other company's testing systems might base the passing score on what people taking the exam prior to you achieved. In the WordPerfect system, the passing score represents a true level of

expertise of the program being tested. It does not fluctuate based upon the results of other people taking the exam.

The remainder of this chapter will introduce you to what topics will be covered on the examinations and give you a brief overview of them. It will point out items to look for when working with the feature.

WordPerfect DOS certified business certification (CBC)

WordPerfect DOS certified business certification (CBC) is an entry-level certification, not intended for advanced support or training professionals. This level of certification is intended to help people demonstrate their competence using the WordPerfect DOS product.

Those people who want to obtain WordPerfect Certified Instructor status need to pass the higher level WordPerfect DOS or Windows Certified Professional Credential (CPC) certification exam. The CBC is not valid when pursuing Certified Instructor status.

WordPerfect DOS certified business certification is achieved by demonstrating that the candidate is capable of using the product to perform a generic series of standard job tasks and has mastered a set of skills. Job tasks that are evaluated at the CBC level include:

- Installing the WordPerfect program
- Customizing the WordPerfect environment
- Managing files

You should be familiar with the product's installation program and able to accurately describe each of the options encountered during installation. You should be able to customize the WordPerfect display and change user preferences such as the location of files. You should understand how to use the File Manager feature to perform all basic DOS operations such as copy, move, print, or delete files with or without opening them.

The skills that are evaluated include the ability to use the features of the product to:

- ➢ Create a form
- ➢ Produce a business letter and envelope
- ➢ Create a memo
- ➢ Create a résumé
- ➢ Produce meeting minutes
- ➢ Create an agenda
- ➢ Design a brochure
- ➢ Create a financial statement
- ➢ Design a newsletter
- ➢ Produce a report

Each one of these abilities calls upon the candidate to demonstrate that he or she knows how to use various features of the product. Creating forms typically involves use of the table feature. The candidate should know how to create and customize tables. When creating business letters, and more importantly envelopes, the candidate would need to be able to change the paper size or type and alter the margins of the page. Memos and résumés also manipulate the margins.

For creating minutes and agendas, the candidate will need to be able to set and use margins. All the other features discussed previously could also be used as each of these skills builds upon others.

Basic use of the desktop publishing features, including the ability to change fonts within a document, are tested by designing a brochure. That same level of difficulty, plus tabular data, could be used to create a financial statement. Using graphics and columns would be vital when designing a newsletter. Finally, page numbering and headers and footers would be important when producing a report.

WordPerfect DOS certified professional certification (CPC)

CPC certification is for professionals engaged in training and support and is a step beyond the CBC (an advanced user level) certification. People who want to obtain WordPerfect Certified Instructor status need to pass the WordPerfect DOS or Windows CPC certification exam. The CBC level of certification is not valid when pursuing Certified Instructor status.

The CPC topics include:

- Setting up WordPerfect
- Managing files
- Formatting documents
- Editing documents
- Automating tasks
- Professional publications
- Tables and spreadsheets
- Special features
- Printing
- Troubleshooting

Setting up WordPerfect

You will have to know about the Installation and Startup procedures. This would include knowing about the minimum hardware and operating system requirements that make the program run. You should know the hardware/software requirements that WordPerfect recommends.

Having an understanding of the different Installation Options that are available to you will be beneficial. Know the difference between

Standard, Custom, and Network Installations. The best way to learn about this is to install WordPerfect three times using the different installation options. If using Custom Installation, try going back into the installation process and adding a feature that you didn't choose the first time around. You should know which files are crucial to make the program run and which files and drivers are not required. You should be familiar with how much disk space the WordPerfect files take up, as well as some Install options.

When you purchase WordPerfect 6.0, you also get WordPerfect Shell version 4.0. Shell lets you arrange programs and commands into a menu structure. You will be required to know how to Install Shell, Create Menus, and how the Clipboard feature works.

You should have experience setting up WordPerfect's Setup Options. You should know how to set up the mouse and display options (graphics versus text mode). The setup environment includes backup options, beep on error, and the like. Ask yourself why you would choose a particular keyboard layout over the others (macros, original, etc.).

Location of Files is setting up the directories for where you want the different program files to be located and where you want the documents to be saved. Although WordPerfect will create these directories if they are not already created on the hard drive, a basic knowledge of how to create, use, and remove DOS subdirectories will be helpful.

Though most faithful users can recognize the familiar WordPerfect display at a glance, virtually every aspect can be changed to suit the user's tastes. This topic covers areas such as defining user preferences for display color (foreground, background, and options) and changing the location of button bars.

Knowledge regarding where to get help when setting up WordPerfect is also important. You should be able to understand the manual conventions in the reference guide. You should understand all the different ways to access the online Help feature. Practice looking up different features first by Contents, Index, and How do I, then try using a feature with the Coaches. If you are a new user, try using the online Tutorial.

Managing files

File Manager is important because this is the area where you have access to your files. It allows you to retrieve, look at, copy, move, rename, delete, or print files. You should be familiar with all the menu options under File Manager. In order to fully understand this section, DOS knowledge is required. Knowledge about filenames, paths, and saving to directories is assumed. File Manager does enable you to accomplish all the DOS tasks (making directories, renaming files, etc.), but understanding the essential elements of DOS will make getting through this section of the test easier.

Understanding the difference between QuickFinder and QuickList is essential. QuickFinder is a timesaving feature that lets you index all words in selected documents, which accelerates any search through those selected documents for words or phrases. You should understand how to create a QuickFinder Index, update the indexes, and regenerate individual indexes, if needed.

QuickList lets you mark files and directories used frequently. Know the keystrokes to call up QuickList (F5,F6). You should know how to add, modify, or remove something from a QuickList.

The document summary feature allows the user to better categorize documents and is an invaluable search tool. You should understand how to set up and select the fields you want for the document summary and how to extract information from the document into the summary fields.

Formatting documents

Certain formatting codes need to be inserted at the top of the current paragraph or page. In order to get the desired formatting result, you should understand how the Autocode placement feature works, which codes are affected by it, and what are the results when the Autocode placement feature is turned off.

You should have an understanding of how to create, edit, and set up the different layout options for footnotes and endnotes. Important elements of Footnotes are setting the spacing between footnotes and the footer separator line options (type of line, length, and alignment). You should know how to renumber endnotes or footnotes manually or format all note numbers at once. You should know how to insert page headers and footers.

What are Watermarks? This feature lets you have images "behind" your document text. It is usually a background for the page. A company logo, clip art, or a special drawing can easily be made into a Watermark. You should be able to create it, move it, and turn it off for subsequent pages. When editing, you should know how to adjust a Watermark's brightness and contrast, rotate it, and reduce or enlarge it.

Styles are a typographical arrangement and display in which text can be set up. If you always bold, italicize, and underline a portion of text, you can save this format in a style so you can easily retrieve this formatting sequence and apply it to other text.

How and why do you use styles? You should be able to distinguish between the different styles: Paragraph, Character, and Open. To learn more about styles, make up a sample newsletter and create different styles for it. Try saving the styles into the style libraries. Know the different types of style libraries that are available (personal and shared); also know how to copy and retrieve styles from libraries into documents. We additionally recommend creating a style from existing codes and text.

You should know how to create different paper sizes or edit the given ones. Try creating a new paper size, naming it, selecting a paper type (letterhead, bond, card stock), and choosing the location of where the paper will be in the printer (sheet feeder, continuous, or manual feed). Do you want to have the program prompt you to load the paper? Consider all these options when setting up new paper sizes or modifying the existing sizes.

If you have mastered paper sizes, setting up envelopes should be simple. The only additional feature to envelopes is being able to understand how to set the address positions. You must have a

knowledge of POSTNET bar codes. The bar code is used by the U.S. Postal Service for mail delivery. Know the different Bar Code Creation options. Do you want the bar code to be automatic or manual?

There are many options to consider when setting up Labels. The key in setting up Labels is to get the text in the exact position that you desire on the label. Label size, number of labels, Top, Left, Corner, distance between labels, margins, and label type are some of the settings you must understand how to use and how they affect the label's appearance.

The WordPerfect Outline feature allows the user to easily create multilevel outline documents. You will need to understand how to edit your outline after it has been created. We suggest creating a simple outline and try changing from one level to another. Change an outline item to normal text. Practice hiding portions of the text in your outline. Show only certain levels of your outline. Know the keystrokes for moving between levels.

Editing documents

You should be familiar with the different ways to move around a document via the keyboard, mouse, or keystrokes. You will need to be familiar with the "Go to" feature and the different locations in the document that it will take you to.

You should understand the concepts of Reveal Codes. Reveal Codes is like going behind the scenes of the program.

When you set a margin, tab, or any keystroke, WordPerfect keeps track of it. When you need to see exactly what feature you put in a document, the Reveal Codes feature will show such things as [Col Def] and you should understand what it means (in this example "Define a Column"). Knowing how revertible codes are put on to blocks of text and what happens when you delete one part of the revertible code is important. You should go into a document in your test directory and look at the codes that were added after you tested out some of the features.

Most users are familiar with an automatic spell checker looking for misspelled words, duplicate words, and certain capitalization errors. Don't forget to review the use of the supplemental dictionaries: what they are, how to create and edit them, and how to chain between a main and supplemental dictionary.

Grammatik is an automatic grammar checker. It can check your document for the different writing levels. You should be familiar with how to use the different automatic checking features.

The Compare Document feature lets you compare two documents; it highlights the differences in the documents. Create one document and save it with two different names. Go into the second document and change a couple of words. Now you will be ready to run Compare Document. Understand how you can change the different markings that are inserted into the document when the comparison is completed.

Automating tasks

The Button Bar feature allows you to have access to features, macros, and other Button Bars that you use frequently. You should know how to create a button bar, how to select the predefined button bars that come with WordPerfect, and how to move the buttons to different locations on the bar.

A macro is a series of WordPerfect instructions executed in a batch. You should be familiar with the syntax of a macro command—when (), {}, and ; are needed. Try recording some simple macros and then going back and editing them. If you run into problems with macros, WordPerfect has an online macros manual that can be found under the Help menu. This lists all the macro commands and system variables available to you when creating macros. Each macro command under Help shows you what the abbreviation, syntax, and parameters should be for that command. You might also be directed where to look for more help.

Merge is used to combine data (called a *data file*) with information in documents (called a *form file*) to mass produce documents such as

labels, envelopes, reports, and letters. You should be comfortable setting up different types of data files. You should review everything about creating the data merge, from naming the fields to setting up the forms. When merging your two files, be aware of all the different output options, data file options, and defining conditions for the merge.

Sort lets you alphabetize text, order numbers, and gives you the opportunity to extract information from a list. You should understand what a record is and the types of records that WordPerfect lets you sort on. You should know how to perform a sort and select the different keys and fields to perform exactly what you want to sort on. Create a simple file that has names and zip codes and try your hand at sorting in different orders and the different fields.

The keyboard's keys are programmed to do certain features. For example, CTRL Z lets you undo a command. Well, you have the opportunity to reprogram CTRL Z to CTRL U if you wanted. You should have an understanding of how to select new keyboard layouts and edit them. You should know what features you can assign to the keystrokes: Commands, Characters, or Macros.

Professional publications

Be familiar with the different types of columns available to you, such as the differences between Newspaper and Parallel columns. You should know how to set column borders, change the width between columns, and move around from column to column.

You should feel comfortable adding borders to paragraphs, pages, or columns in your document. You should be able to add shading to a border, change the border's line style or color, and be able to adjust the inside and outside spacing of a border.

Master documents let you control large documents. You should understand how to create a master document by inserting the subdocuments. You should know how to expand and condense the master document. You should understand what formatting codes will be in effect when you make formatting changes to either the master document or the subdocuments.

WordPerfect Index features can create a list of items and generate the page number where the items can be found, such as a book's index. You should know the steps to mark specific text items for an index and how to generate the index.

Cross-References will make notations to refer readers from one place to another for pertinent information. You will need to be familiar with how to mark the reference location and the target that you are referencing.

 Tables and spreadsheets

Tables are presentations of data in rows and columns. When you set information up in a table, in some cases it is easier than setting tabs and trying to align data. You'll need to understand how to create a table and move throughout the table. The Table Edit Mode is the key to changing the table structure. You'll need to know how to add and delete rows and columns. You'll need to know how to put on lines and borders.

You can put mathematical formulas in a WordPerfect table that lets your table have spreadsheet capabilities. You should know about Arithmetic and Logical Operators and what characters represent addition, subtraction, multiplication, and division: respectively +, –, *, and /. You should be able to create formulas also using logical operators: &(AND), !(NOT), ¦(OR), and the like. You should understand the Order of operation, which refers to what operations take precedence in a mathematical formula. Simple mathematics will be helpful for this section.

If you have created a spreadsheet in another program, WordPerfect lets you import it into your current document. You should know which program formats are supported. You can also create a link between your spreadsheet file and your WordPerfect document. By having a link when you update a number in the spreadsheet, it automatically updates the number in your WordPerfect document.

The following is an example of a possible test question that WordPerfect might ask about tables. This question was prepared by WordPerfect Corporation's Certification Department.

When modifying the following table, you select the shaded cell and change the left line of the cell to Default. Why will the line still appear Thick? (Item Type: Multiple Choice)

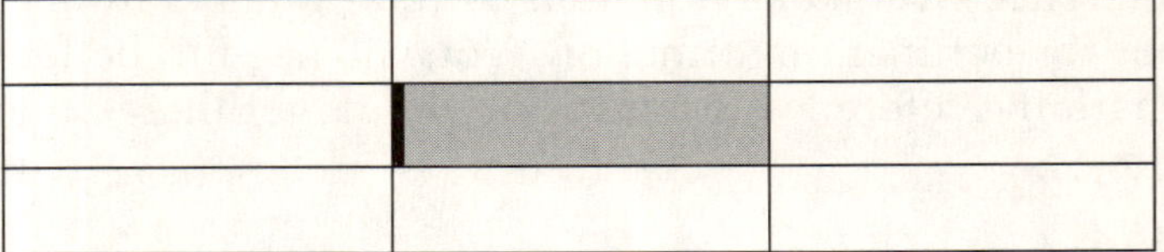

A. The Default line style is Thick.

B. Once a line has been changed to Thick, it cannot be changed back.

C. There is a Thick line at the right side of the adjacent cell.

D. You need to change the Inside lines to Single.

E. You need to change the Border lines to Default.

The correct answer is choice C. There is a Thick line at the right side of the adjacent cell.

Special features

Keyboards do not have certain characters, for instance, ¶, Σ, and É, but there are occasions when you need these symbols. Using the Compose Feature will allow you to use these symbols in your documents. You should be familiar with calling up the WordPerfect character sets and inserting these symbols.

WordPerfect is used throughout the world and therefore has the program available in different languages. You'll need to know how to set up WordPerfect and select another language module through the Setup/Environment feature.

Sound Clips will let you produce multimedia documents for presentations. You should understand what type of sound files can be used and how a clip is inserted into a document.

WordPerfect includes a facsimile capability that allows the user to print a document through a fax modem over the telephone lines to a remote fax machine. You should know how this capability works including the TSR (terminate and stay resident) programs that must be loaded for the feature to work. You can also define a phone book of frequently called fax numbers; you should be able to maintain that fax list.

The Bookmark feature allows a user to mark a specific spot in a document so that he or she can return to that point quickly. You should know how to set and then return to a bookmark.

The new Hypertext features of WordPerfect allow the user to create a button in a document that, when activated, moves the reader to another part of the document. The Hypertext feature uses bookmarks, and you should know how to create, edit, and delete a Hypertext link.

The equation editor allows a user to take full advantage of the extended WordPerfect character set in order to create and edit scientific and math equations. You need to know how to create an equation using the equation editor.

Printing

The WordPerfect program directly supports hundreds of printers through the printer driver files that ship with the product. You should be familiar with defining printers during installation and understand how to add a new printer to a existing installation. You'll need to know how to use the special features of various printers to handle special-size paper, envelopes, and sheet-feed attachments.

WordPerfect is shipped with a variety of fonts that can be used to personalize documents. Which font is used by default and how can that be changed? How can you change the size and appearance (bold, underline, italics) of a font? You should know how to use these fonts within a document and how to add new fonts to your system.

A variety of options are available for printing documents, such as printing the entire document, printing a selected range, and printing only the even- or odd-numbered pages. You need to know how all the print options work and understand how to use WordPerfect to control the printer.

Troubleshooting

Under the heading "general troubleshooting," most WordPerfect users report confusion with documents being "lost" because they are unclear about the location of files. Although it is a setup issue, the ability to determine where WordPerfect is currently looking for various types of files is important.

You'll need to understand some reasons why you could be experiencing printing problems. Is your printer hardware connected properly? Is the WordPerfect software set up correctly? Most printing problems can be traced back to the installation of the correct and the current version of the printer driver.

You should know how to check how much memory a computer has available. You should know the WordPerfect requirements for memory before installing and running WordPerfect applications.

WordPerfect InForms Certified Professional Credential (CPC)

The WordPerfect InForms Certified Professional Credential (CPC) is intended for advanced users and form designers. These users would typically use the product in a nonnetworked environment or rely on a network professional to install and maintain the product on a

network. The CPC exam tests the candidate's capabilities to use the product to create and distribute InForms documents from a stand-alone or single workstation environment.

People who want to obtain InForms Certified Instructorr status need to pass one of the InForms certification exams, either CPC or CSE.

Topics include:

- Form layout
- Links
- Calculations
- Distribution
- Query and report

When working with InForms the person who develops the form is the designer, and the person who fills in or completes the form is the user.

Form layout

There are three basic components to the program: form designer, form filler, and form security programs. Each has its own Windows interface, and you should understand how each is used. The security program is used almost exclusively in a networked environment.

Form objects are parts of a form that allow the user to input data. You should know what the different form objects are and how to use each form object. Graphics objects are used to add graphic elements to a form. These objects are usually for display or reference purposes only. You should know how graphics objects can be used. Object libraries allow the designer to take a form or graphic object or a group of objects and save the object or objects to disk for later reuse.

Graphics files can be added or linked to an InForms document. You should know what types of graphics files can be used and how to include them into the document.

InForms documents can be completed by the user in one of two ways, either by filling in a printed form or electronically on a computer. Many tradeoffs and design decisions need to be made, depending upon the user's method to fill in the form.

Links

When a user completes an InForms document electronically, the designer can use the linking features to either help the user work through the form or record the information into a text or database file. You should be familiar with each of the different types of links that can be created and specifically how InForms can be used to enter data into a database file and which database file formats are supported.

Calculations

Designers can create forms that perform calculations based upon information from a user. You need to know what types of calculations can be performed. InForms includes a number of predefined math functions, and you need to know what they are and how to use them.

Query and report

An online form can also be used to look up information from a database. When users are searching for information in a database, they typically either are looking for a specific piece of information (also called a *query*), or they want to know all the records in the database that match certain input criteria and subsequently see the result in the form of a report.

Distribution

Online InForms documents can be completed with the InForms filer. These files can be copied onto a diskette and given to the user, or they can be delivered via an electronic mail system, such as

WordPerfect Office. You should understand the basic concepts behind distributing forms over a network, including compatible mail systems and the type of InForms file that would need to be generated.

WordPerfect InForms certified System Engineer (CSE)

The WordPerfect InForms Certified System Engineer (CSE) is intended for advanced network users and form designers working in a network environment. Where the CPC level of certification called for basic knowledge of how to create and distribute forms in a network environment, the CSE credential requires knowledge of the network system. The CSE exam tests the candidate's capabilities to use the product to create, distribute, and secure InForms documents from a network environment.

People who want to obtain InForms Certified Instructor status need to pass one of the InForms certification exams, either CPC or CSE.

It is advised that anyone pursuing CSE certification have a solid working knowledge of a network operating system like Novell's NetWare, Banyan Vines, or Microsoft LAN Manager. For a more complete and up-to-date list of the network operating systems supported, see the product documentation.

The CSE exam covers many of the same topics as the CPC exam including:

- Form layout
- Links
- Calculations
- Distribution
- Query and report

The reader should refer to the WordPerfect InForms Certified Professional Credential (CPC) section in this chapter for more information about those topics.

Topics specific to the InForms CSE exam include:

- Stand-alone machine
- Network system
- Security

 Stand-alone machine

The stand-alone machine is an InForms station that is not connected to a network. You need to know the basic hardware and software system requirements for configuration of a computer, such as PC. What InForms files would be installed on a nonnetworked PC? Does the stand-alone user need all the InForms files? What are the defaults set up after the InForms product is installed, such as the locations of directories and files? As a Windows application, what Windows files are changed during an InForms installation?

 Network System

How is the InForms product installed in a network environment? What network types are supported? You need to know the basic hardware and software system requirements for configuring InForms in the network. What InForms files would be installed on a file server versus a workstation PC? Does the network user need all the InForms files? Where are the InForms file stored on a network?

After the InForms product is installed on the network, the network provides a much easier way to move the files from user to user. Where the CPC designer needed to know the basics of how to move InForms documents, the CSE needs to know some level of detail, including the specific file types and the electronic mail systems supported.

Security

The security feature allows the designer to create portions of a form that cannot be completed except by authorized personnel. This feature also defines electronic signatures that allow for the secure handling and routing of electronic documents. CSE candidates need to know how to use these features.

WordPerfect Office/Novell GroupWise Certified System Engineer (CSE)

WordPerfect Office/Novell GroupWise Certified System Engineer (CSE) certification is an advanced certification intended for advanced support or training professionals. This level of certification is intended for LAN system integrators and support professionals as well as people wishing to train users and administrators of the WordPerfect Office/Novell GroupWise product.

As stated earlier for the InForms CSE certification, it is advised that anyone pursuing CSE certification have a solid working knowledge of a network operating system such as Novell's NetWare, Banyan Vines, or Microsoft LAN Manager. For a more complete and up-to-date list of the network operating systems supported, see the product documentation.

People who want to pursue WordPerfect Office/Novell GroupWise Certified Instructor status need to pass the WordPerfect Office/Novell GroupWise CSE certification exam.

Topics include:

- Planning
- Installation
- Maintenance

- Troubleshooting
- Generic gateways and cross platforms
- Asynchronous gateway
- WordPerfect office remote

Planning

In order to implement an electronic mail system using WordPerfect Office/Novell GroupWise, you'll need to know the general architecture of a mail system. Office mail systems are comprised of *domains*.

A domain is an electronic mail system that contains post offices, which in turn contain users's mail boxes. A domain is the largest unit of an Office system and can be as small as a single post office running on a small LAN to as large as all the file server computers on all the LANs at a multibuilding corporate office.

Larger organizations with multiple locations separated by wide areas would probably have multiple domains. Domains can be linked to one another through the use of message servers and gateways.

A post office is a smaller unit that defines where mail boxes reside. An administrator generally has control over one or more post offices.

Message servers move information between post offices and between domains. A *gateway* is a computer that connects a domain on one LAN to another domain via a special connection. This might be so that users can retrieve their mail while on the road or at home. These are generally referred to as *remote users*. A gateway might be used to connect a small regional office to headquarters. Gateways can also be used to connect Office mail systems on different types of LANs.

For the certification exam, you need to be able to assess the user requirements and make suggestions as to how many domains, post offices, message servers, and gateways are needed. You'll also need

to know the specific requirements that are necessary when linking to different LAN operating systems or remote users.

Installation

You will need to know what the minimum and suggested hardware configuration for each of the possible WordPerfect Office/Novell GroupWise stations (user workstation, message server, gateway). You should be familiar with how much disk space the files will take up on a file server's hard disk.

It is assumed that all candidates have installed the WordPerfect Office/Novell GroupWise product at least once. You should know how to install the WordPerfect Office/Novell GroupWise product and what the installation options are. You should also know how to install a message server and an asynchronous gateway.

The WordPerfect Office administrator uses the ADMIN program (that program's filename is AD.EXE) to administer the Office system. You must know how to add, change, and delete user accounts within a post office using the ADMIN program. It is important to know which fields of a user's personal information are required and which fields are optional.

Maintenance

An important part of maintaining the mail system is knowing how and where (in the subdirectory structure) Office stores program, user, and mail message files. It is important that you be able to determine the path a message would follow through the directory structure to be delivered to another user.

The WordPerfect Office ADMIN program allows for the administrator who is responsible for the domain to make changes. These changes are then passed to each of the post offices within the domain. How often and how quickly does that happen? What happens if an employee transfers within the department and you need to relocate

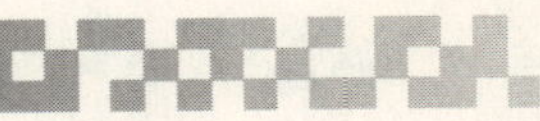

them to a another post office within the same domain? How can this be accomplished?

Troubleshooting

Most troubleshooting tasks in a mail system involve trying to determine why messages fail to arrive. That's why it is very important that you understand message flow through the subdirectory structure. Many of these problems that involve the failure of mail to properly flow through the system can be solved easily by correcting the path another program is looking at for messages or by making sure that the network is allowing the mail user with proper rights to read from that portion of the directory structure. (A user's ability to access portions of a network directory structure is determined by the user's *rights*.)

Another common type of troubleshooting involves solving printing problems. You should be familiar with how print jobs are handled both by the WordPerfect Office/Novell GroupWise product and the network operating system.

Generic gateways and cross platforms

You will need to understand how to help users who are using the older WordPerfect Office 3.1 mail system communicate with and upgrade to an Office 4.0 system. A key point is understanding the differences between the 3.1 and 4.0 Office products and understanding how to create an environment where they can interchange messages.

WordPerfect Office supports several commercially popular and worldwide mail exchange standards. You need to know the basics of configuring a gateway to exchange mail with a foreign (non-WordPerfect Office) mail system.

Another important point: What happens to the organization of post offices and domains if the company's corporate structure changes?

You need to understand the basic concept of merging two mail systems or dividing (releasing) mail systems.

Asynchronous gateway

An asynchronous gateway allows a WordPerfect Office/Novell GroupWise system to communicate with other Office systems via a dial-up telephone line. You should be familiar with how to install and configure an asynchronous gateway.

WordPerfect Office Remote

WordPerfect Office users can access their mail from mobile (portable) PCs away from their normal office via WordPerfect Office Remote. You should know how to configure the post office mail system, the asynchronous gateway, and the remote user's software.

5

How to prepare

Based upon our experience, the best way to prepare for the certification examination is to spend as much time with your hands on the product learning to use each of the features that you'll be tested on. Exactly how you do this and how long it will take depends upon the preparation option you choose.

We have profiled three different ways to prepare for the certification tests. One way to prepare is on your own, or self-study. Self-study involves obtaining the product and installing it on a computer or computer network, then following the lessons detailed in the manuals or creating your lessons from the product materials.

Another way to prepare is to purchase a study kit, either from WordPerfect Corporation or from a third-party training company. Each kit is literally a course-in-a-box that you complete section by section.

We'll also look at taking a course at a WordPerfect authorized training center. A training center might have the highest initial cost, but you can take full advantage of the instructor's experience and center's hardware.

Self-study

Of all the ways to prepare for a WordPerfect certification examination, self-study seems as though it would be the least expensive. This isn't always true for everyone. We assume that you own or have access to a computer if you are pursuing CBC or CPC certification, or a computer network if you want to achieve CSE or ECSE.

A wide variety of books about WordPerfect products are available in bookstores. Having a good reference book, other than the WordPerfect manual, should be a requirement for everyone seeking certification.

May I use a reference book to study for the certification exam? The short answer is "Yes and no." While many of the reference books for WordPerfect provide valuable information about the product, they don't present the information in such a way as to help you learn how to use the features to solve a problem. They simply present feature after feature of the software in a reference format.

The same statement can be made about many of the videotapes that are commercially available. We have looked at several of the best videos and found that if you want to learn how to use WordPerfect from scratch—assuming that you have little computer knowledge or little knowledge of office skills, such as writing a business letter—some of these videos can be very helpful. Most videos do group several related features together to demonstrate how they are used. We did not find that they went into the level of detail required by the certification examinations.

You also need access to the product that you want to certify on. "Borrowing a copy" of the software is illegal, and the software copyright laws are not to be taken lightly. *Use a legal copy of the product.* All Certified Instructors are asked the serial number of the products they used to prepare.

If you choose to self-study, you have to have discipline. You have to motivate yourself to work with the product and explore the features. Creating your own course of study that is based upon what you know can take much longer than either using a kit or taking a course.

Each WordPerfect and InForms product comes with an online tutorial and a series of lessons in the manual. You should know the entire tutorial before attempting the examination. The lessons are great practice, and you should create your own new lessons using these as a basis.

Studying for the Office/GroupWise examination is much harder because of the amount of time needed to set up and experiment with the product.

Study kit

While we were developing this book, the only study materials that were commercially available were from WordPerfect Corporation. If

you are considering purchasing self-study materials (a courseware kit), you will probably consider books from several different vendors. We suggest that you use our descriptions as a means of comparing the WordPerfect materials with those of another vendor.

WordPerfect Corporation currently offers the following courseware kits:

- WordPerfect 6.0 DOS Professional Skills Study Kit
- WordPerfect 6.0 DOS Business Skills Study Kit
- WordPerfect 6.0 DOS Essential Skills Study Kit
- WordPerfect 6.0 Windows Professional Skills Study Kit
- WordPerfect 6.0 Windows Business Skills Study Kit
- WordPerfect Office/Novell GroupWise 4.0 System Engineer Skills
- WordPerfect InForms 1.0 System Engineer Skills (includes Designer Skills Study Kit)
- WordPerfect InForms 1.0 Form Designer Skills Study Kit

WordPerfect has also developed a series of "transitional" courseware packages to make it easier to learn WordPerfect by using examples from other similar software.

All courseware kits come with a study guide and a practice certification examination. The study guide is similar (in most cases the same) to the classroom materials. The study guide is a printed manual designed to help you thoroughly practice using important product features.

All study guides are broken down into three sections:

- Job Tasks or Projects
- Feature Modules
- Practice Tests

The Job Tasks are practice lessons in which you are given a job to perform and you have to go through the steps to complete it. This would almost be equivalent to a request from your employer to

"Please make some sense out of this for my proposal to the new client." The lesson gives you clues as to features you might want to use to accomplish this task. Sometimes the Job Task assignments require you to retrieve a file from the diskette that is supplied with the study kit.

If you run into problems in the Job Task section, you can refer to the Features Module section where you will be guided through how to use the feature. The Features Module section is more for the individual who knows the feature is available but hasn't used it.

The study guide also contains a glossary of terms (see the glossary of this book) and an appendix with the sample certification test questions (part 4 of this book).

WordPerfect Corporation has experimented with a variety of ways of delivering course material via computer, rather than printing manuals. CAVIS (Comprehensive Assessment-Validated Instruction System) is an online tool developed for WordPerfect 6.0 for DOS that was provided on a floppy diskette as part of the kit. In order to run CAVIS for WordPerfect 6.0 DOS, you will need WordPerfect 6.0 for DOS installed on your computer. The CAVIS package includes a course curriculum, learning files, and a practice test for the WordPerfect 6.0 DOS product only.

WordPerfect has not developed a CAVIS system for other products such as WordPerfect for Windows 6.0, InForms, and Office. (The company is developing new online learning systems for those products.) The current online curriculum for Office and InForms is a series of online documents accessed via Folio Views, a text search and retrieval program. Folio Views is discussed in more detail in chapter 6, in the WordPerfect INFOBASE section; portions of INFOBASE are supplied with each different type of student kit.

The practice certification examinations are a good way to test yourself and your study and preparation progress. The practice tests closely resemble what the actual certification examinations will be like. We suggest that you spend as much time as necessary and complete all the practice examinations before attempting an official certification examination.

The practice test is similar to the performance-based computer test that you will be taking to become certified. The practice test is broken down into different sections that you will be tested on. The system scores your correct answers. The test can be taken numerous times, but only your last score is recorded.

When using the practice test on WordPerfect 6.0 DOS, you can actually perform a requested task by selecting the option "Do it in 6.0," which takes you out of the test-question mode and puts you on a blank document screen.

Training center course

Many people choose to prepare for an examination by taking a course at an authorized training center. Courses are taught by people who have passed the examinations at WordPerfect-authorized training centers. The corporation authorizes training centers that have the required hardware and software needed to help candidates prepare.

While this option might seem like the most expensive, you don't have to concern yourself with owning a copy of the software or even a computer. For many people who want to achieve CSE certification, it gives you the opportunity to experiment on a network. Many LAN administrators are afraid that their actions might disrupt normal business on their employer's LAN; therefore, the opportunity for experimentation at the learning center is hard to pass up.

At WordPerfect authorized training centers, several classes are available to help individuals prepare for the examinations. The training classes also include the WordPerfect Study Kits. All classes are hands-on and run between 2–4 days depending upon the class. A list of certification training centers is available from WordPerfect's Certification Department at the phone number listed in appendix B.

Courses available

WordPerfect Office/Novell GroupWise 4.0 System Engineer

This is a 3-day course designed for system integrators and network administrators with advanced knowledge of the network operating system and mail system. The following modules are integrated into realistic scenarios that are comparable with the real-life job situations faced daily by certified System Engineers in the field:

- Overview
- Architecture
- Install
- Multiple Host
- Multiple Domain
- Remote Office/Asynchronous Gateways
- Host Convert

InForms 1.0 System Engineer

This is a 3-day course designed for system integrators and network administrators with advanced knowledge of the network operating system and mail systems. Each of the following modules will be integrated into a realistic enterprise, comparable to situations faced daily by Certified System Engineers in the field:

- Form Design
- Form Links
- Security/Signatures
- Database Links
- Mail/Transport
- Calculations
- Filler/Query

InForms Designer

This is a 2-day course to learn WordPerfect InForms 1.0 Designer; Designer is a portion of the InForms product. Students will design forms and create a common database for Query. This course will also include advanced features such as Tool Palette and Object Library.

WordPerfect 6.0 Professional Credential

This is a 3-day course that includes the following job-task modules:

- ➢ Agendas
- ➢ Custom screen layout
- ➢ WordPerfect installation
- ➢ Shell setup
- ➢ File management
- ➢ Financial statements
- ➢ Forms
- ➢ Letters/envelopes
- ➢ Minutes
- ➢ Newsletters
- ➢ Reports
- ➢ Resumes
- ➢ Troubleshooting

Before you take a course at a training center, ask about the instructor and the hardware that will be made available for your use in class. The process of becoming a Certified Instructor is very rigorous. All instructors have had to pass the examination at either the CPC or CSE level. The level of quality control actively enforced by WordPerfect Corporation's certification department is also very demanding.

You might want to find out about other certifications held by the instructor. For example, if you're seeking to learn about how WordPerfect Office works in a Novell-networked environment, it would be useful if your instructor were certified to teach WordPerfect and Novell.

While all WordPerfect-Certified Instructors are knowledgeable, the type of computer hardware available in the training center can vary widely. Make sure that the equipment that the center uses is similar or better than your own. Many centers have classrooms equipped with the latest, most powerful computers. Will the product you're learning about run the same way on your equipment? You might encounter significant problems or extreme difficulties if the training is on an older and less powerful PC than what you will be working on.

Certification checklists

The following checklists will come in handy when trying to prepare for the different examinations. You should spend a reasonable amount of time on the different topics. Study by using the practice materials and study guides or working with the product.

Studying for the examination can be very overwhelming. You need to look at the test subject breakdown and go from there. You should also keep track of the sections and features when you have reviewed them and work with a checklist. (Checklists are at the end of this chapter.)

Because you can use many resources to study for the examination, the checklists will prevent redundant study and review of identical information. Make sure that you write down your strengths and weaknesses (what you did well and what you barely knew). Nothing is worse than settling in at the test center to take the examination and suddenly realizing that you forgot to study a crucial element.

Underneath the "Time Studied" checklist item, you might want to make note if you think you need to spend more time on that topic. Underneath "Score/Questions," write down your practice examination score and how many of your answers were correct. Use the remaining portions of the checklist to note questions or problems that were encountered when working with that feature.

Preparing for the test

No matter how you choose to prepare for the examination, you need to have a thorough knowledge and performance-based expertise of the product that you are testing on. You have had limited use of the program if your knowledge and use has been concentrated or geared toward a particular feature. You should have a thorough knowledge of the *entire program* before attempting to take a certification test.

Know what comes with the program

We strongly recommend that before you attempt to take a certification examination you should know what comes with the WordPerfect product that you are testing on. What is the product capable of doing? Even if you believe that you have mastered the program, you still need to understand features that you don't use that frequently.

Plan when you want to take the test

Ask yourself when you want to take the certification examination. If you plan on taking it in two months, set up a daily study schedule with specific timeframes for crucial topics. Study when there is the least likelihood of interruptions. Stick to the schedule. This is a lot easier said than done, but you need to start somewhere.

Install the program on your computer

Before you go any further, you should be sitting at a computer. If you haven't already installed the program, this is your opportunity to do so. You should make a separate directory on your computer called "test" to save all practice documents; after you pass the examination, cleaning up the study files will be easier.

When you have gone through the installation process, you are ready to begin trying the different features. When you come to a feature

that you have never used, you should make up a sample document that uses that feature. When working on a feature, task, or skill, place your emphasis on fully utilizing that particular function. You will need to know that function's limitations.

Very important note: Ask yourself why you would use this program function.

If you are very comfortable using specific features of a program, you can spend less time studying them but don't ignore them completely. Make sure that you do a quick review of that feature by going over *all the options* available on the screen. You might also want to check the reference manual and see if it offers any tips or tricks that you might need to know for that feature.

Using the reference manual as a study tool

How do you learn a feature you never used? The WordPerfect Reference Manual will explain all the capabilities of that feature. It will tell you how to call up that feature, via keystrokes or from the pull-down menus. It also gives helpful hints and things to look out for. It tells you about the different options that you might see listed on the screen in the process of setting up that feature. Once you have an understanding of what this feature can do, make up a practice example in a blank document to test it out.

Most WordPerfect products come with a learning manual

If you need help preparing examples, you can use the *Learning WordPerfect Manual* examples as substitutes. If you do not already have this manual, you can get it directly from WordPerfect; documentation for the application includes an order card to request a copy of the learning manual free of charge. Do the lesson that pertains to the respective topic.

Use the online Help feature

If turning to manuals scares you, you may use the online Help menu within the program. Look up the feature on the Help menu and read through the screens, then go back to your blank document and set up your example.

WordPerfect 6.0 for DOS comes with an online tutorial that is broken down into different lessons. It gives you step-by-step instructions on the screen for a given example. You can work on a particular lesson or jump to a topic within one of the lessons. Under Help there is also a feature called Coaches, which does not have many menu options but does exactly what the name claims; it coaches you through different features.

Common questions about examination preparations

How can I be sure I'm using the correct version of the software?

In general, the certification tests do not include questions with answers that are directly affected by the minor upgrade of a product. That means that if you have version 4.0a or 4.01 of the product, you should take the examination for product version 4.

How often do the examinations change?

Changes to the examinations can be made on a daily basis by the WordPerfect Certification Department. The key point is that any examination is a sampling of questions from a large database of questions. If you know someone else who took the examination and they tell you about the hardest questions on their examination, there is no guarantee that those questions will be on your examination the next day.

How often are the tests updated?

Tests are updated when a major update or release of the program is available to the public. Authorized training centers are generally notified in advance to give them time to upgrade facilities and materials.

How will I know I'm ready?

Only you will know when you are ready. Unfortunately, some people know the material very well but don't pass. They just couldn't arrive at the correct answers for the questions they were asked.

Fortunately, you can take the examinations as many times as you need to pass. There is no limit on the number of attempts to pass a certification examination, but you still have to pay for each attempt.

Good luck!

WordPerfect Office 4.0 Exam CSE

Section	Time Studied	Score/Questions
Planning		
Installation		
Maintenance		
Troubleshooting		
Conversion		
ASYNC gateway		
Office remote		
Generic gateway		

WordPerfect InForms 1.0 Exam CPC

Section	Time Studied	Score/Questions
Query & Report		
Distribution		
Calculations		
Links		
Form layout		

WordPerfect InForms 1.0 CSE

	Time Studied	Score/Questions
System Administration:		
Security		
Network system		
Stand-alone machine		
Creation, distribution, and use of forms:		
Query and report		
Distribution		
Calculations		
Links		
Form layout		

WordPerfect 6.0 for DOS CPC

	Time Studied	Score/Questions
Setting Up WordPerfect		
Managing files		
Formatting documents		
Editing documents		
Automating tasks		
Professional publications		
Tables/spreadsheets		
Special features		
Printing		
Troubleshooting		

Registration and examination

CHAPTER 6

Certification requires that an applicant pass a timed computer-based examination. This chapter will explain registering for and taking the examination. We will explain how much time you have to take the test. We will tell you about steps that you should follow to take the examination, and give you insight as to what is happening behind the scenes. In the event that you do not pass, we will tell you about the strategy that we use to turn a loss into a win.

One important point about certification testing is that you shouldn't cheat. Don't even think about cheating, no matter how smart you think you are or how sure you are that you won't get caught. The immediate penalty for being suspected of cheating is that the test doesn't count. The testing centers must report suspected cheating to the testing company. The worst-case scenario is that the testing company or WordPerfect might bar you from taking the test again. Then you'll never be able to get certified, no matter how hard you work.

Cheating is very impractical because the tests are performance-based. Remember that performance-based testing means that they are testing you based on the premise you have worked with the product. No documentation or reference material that you could take into the examination is going to help you answer the questions in the time allotted. Experience is your only resource.

All tests are *proctored*, which means that someone is observing the testing room at all times. A proctor might be in the room or watching through a window or via video camera.

Testing companies

WordPerfect certification examinations are administered by two separate companies, Sylvan Learning Centers and Drake Training and Technologies. Neither is owned by or associated with WordPerfect Corporation. Sylvan and Drake are independent testing companies that have developed an international network of testing centers.

Most of the testing centers are located at training centers operated by other companies (not Sylvan, Drake, or WordPerfect). Most of these companies are in the training business and operate testing centers as a service for their training customers. Sylvan and Drake companies operate a number of their own testing centers throughout the country and internationally.

Both companies administer examinations for a variety of companies and organizations other than WordPerfect. Other certification examinations might involve computer companies such as Sun Microsystems, Compaq, and Novell; licensing examinations might be administered for the Federal Aviation Administration, Federal Communications Commission, and various professional organizations.

Registration

Call each testing company to locate the center nearest you. Sylvan Learning Centers can be reached at 800-869-1100, and Drake Training and Technology can be reached at 800-2WP-EXAM (800-297-3926). You might have to wait on hold for a few minutes if you call during a busy time of the day.

Ask the customer representative for the location and hours of operation of the testing center nearest you. The representative will usually request your city and state, then read a list of nearby testing centers. Some centers do not administer examinations every weekday; therefore, verify the examination hours at each center.

In general, Drake claims that a candidate should not have to drive more than an hour from his or her home to take the examination. Both companies have extensive testing networks nationally and internationally.

The process of registering for the examination is really simple. When you are sure that you have adequately prepared for the examination, call the testing company to register. The testing companies can typically schedule your examination for the same day you call; however, we recommend that you schedule the examination at least two days in advance. A slight delay gives you some extra time to study some more before the examination and focus on the task.

When you call to schedule the examination, the representative of the testing company will request your:

- ➢ Name
- ➢ Address
- ➢ Date of birth
- ➢ Daytime and possibly evening telephone numbers
- ➢ The test name or number that you wish to register for
- ➢ Your form of payment

You should let the representative know if you are retaking an examination after an unsuccessful attempt. WordPerfect charges significantly less for retakes, up to 30 percent less than the cost of the original test.

In addition, in the United States, the representative will ask for your social security number. Note that both companies use a candidate's social security number as a testing identification number. Options are available if for any reason you do not want to divulge your social security number or if you are a candidate from outside the United States. Sylvan will generate a test identification code using your birth date and last name; Drake will generate a random test identification number.

Payment for certification examinations is made by either using a major credit card or testing company account, or by obtaining a test voucher. Most major credit cards are accepted. Large companies that have many people testing on a regular basis can set up an account with the testing company. Test vouchers can usually be purchased at the testing center; contact the center directly for further information regarding vouchers.

Make sure that you have this information ready before you call. As mentioned earlier, there are sometimes brief delays getting through to a testing company. Delays are most often caused by people taking longer than necessary to register for an examination.

It is very important that the information you give to the testing company representative is correct. WordPerfect Corporation gets your name and address and other information from the testing company's computer.

The testing company will give you an appointment for a date and time to take the examination at the testing center. It is sometimes impossible for the representative to schedule the examination for the exact time that you want because of factors such as testing center hours, other tests that were previously scheduled, and the test length.

After the scheduling is completed, the testing company must ensure that the testing center receives your examination. The process of getting the test information to the test center starts with your phone call to make an appointment for the test. After your test request has been entered into the testing company's computer by the representative, the computer puts your test information into a schedule of all other people taking tests at that center.

Every evening, a computer located at each testing center calls the testing company's computer, usually in the middle of the night when the phone rates are low and the telephone lines aren't busy. When the computers connect, the testing center's computer sends all the results of that day's tests up to the testing company's computer, which is called *uploading*. The testing company computer then sends down the next day's tests to the testing center, which is called *downloading*.

Test day

Arrive at the testing center at or slightly before the scheduled appointment time. If you think you are going to be late, call to make sure that the testing center can still accommodate you that day. Note: If you miss your examination, the testing company will not refund your money unless there are extremely extenuating and documented circumstances.

At the testing center, you should get comfortable. Most testing centers will ask you to hang up your coat because they don't want you to take it into the testing room. Do not bring a briefcase or portfolio of any kind with you. If you do, you will probably be asked to leave it with the test administrator before you go into the testing room. Ladies are generally permitted to bring their purse or handbag.

All WordPerfect tests are closed-book and do not require the use of a calculator, so leave it at home. Perhaps the best place for any last-minute-cramming study materials that you used is in the car, not in the testing center's reception room.

You will be asked to sign in before you enter the testing room. The sign-in process involves producing two forms of identification and entering your signature in the testing center's logbook. You can use your driver's license, social security card, work identification, or credit cards. One form of identification should have a photo. The test administrator will verify and record the information about your identification on the sign-in sheet.

Most test administrators will not record your credit card numbers on the sign-in sheet because people that sign in after you would have an opportunity to view your credit card number. If you are uncomfortable supplying that information, you should arrange to have an alternate form of identification with you that day.

The test

You will be shown to one of several testing stations in the testing room. Other candidates might be taking tests, so try not to make any noise or bother them. The testing station will have the computer, a pad of paper, and a pen or pencil to write with. Stricter testing centers will give you only two pieces of paper and a pen or pencil.

The test administrator will then log you into the testing system and get the station ready to load your test. If there is any problem with the computer you are using before or during the test, you should stop

immediately and notify the administrator. Before the test commences, ask about specific actions to take if there is a malfunction.

Some test administrators will walk you to your seat, let you sit down, and then immediately start your test. It is usually a good idea to inform the administrator that you do not want the test to start until you are ready to start, which gives you a few minutes to relax, settle down, focus on the task at hand, and write down any last-minute notes.

If a particular topic was troublesome during your preparation, write down any crucial points that will help you during the test. *Remember, you will not be allowed to remove your notes from the testing area after the examination.*

Before the examination starts, you'll be asked to complete a survey about how you prepared for the test. The survey helps WordPerfect Corporation improve the study materials and hopefully the examination. It takes about 4 or 5 minutes and should be an excellent opportunity to help you become more relaxed.

When taking the test, don't be concerned about the amount of time that is left before the examining session ends. Each WordPerfect examination is designed to take 1–2 hours to complete. The period allotted for your examination usually allows most people to finish in ample time. The testing companies generally add at least 15 minutes to the length to give you time before and after your test.

Please be absolutely quiet when you are in the testing room. Do not talk to yourself and do not read the questions out loud, either of which distracts others and might cause a disqualification. Never talk to other people in the testing room; if other people talk to you, ignore them. If the testing room is noisy because of someone talking, people in the hall, construction, and the like, get the attention of the administrator and ask him or her to have the noise or distraction stopped.

Remember to read each question carefully before answering. Many people read the question and then select the first answer that "looks" correct. The examination writers usually build in *distracters*, which are wrong answers that are designed for you to immediately read and

think are correct. Read the question and *all the possible answers*. Eliminate the bad answers on scratch paper or in your head.

Before moving on to the next question, silently read the question and your answer one more time to make sure that everything makes sense.

Candidates should be especially aware of the use of negatives, such as "which of the following is NOT a reason." Also, be very careful when answering the multi-multiple choice questions to make sure that you've selected all of the answers you believe are correct.

If there is a serious problem with the testing system workstation—perhaps the system is "hanging" or freezing, or the power goes out—immediately stand up and get the administrator. The test center software is designed to save your answers before moving to the next question. The test administrator should be able to resume your test after correcting the problem. In the event of a power failure, when the electricity returns, the test-system software will usually restart the test at the same question that you were answering when the power went out.

As you take the examination, you might want to make notes about the questions that you had a problem with. Do not take the time to write down the complete question, but you should note the particular topic or answer that proved difficult. You will not be able to keep these notes after the examination, but the notations will help you assess your performance before leaving the testing room. This is especially important if you don't pass. (Just as you might have jotted down a few notes immediately before the test began, perhaps you could memorize a few key terms from troublesome topics and jot down those terms as soon as you leave the testing center.)

Another important note about the answers to test questions: Many people who fail the examination try to figure out every answer on every question. Remember that you should concentrate on understanding the questions. It is very frustrating when you go back to your books or your instructor and try to find the question where the answer is X.

 The results

When the test is over, the results will be displayed on the testing station monitor. Take your time and read the results because there is valuable information here. Before you leave the room, review your written notes and try to assess which areas of the examination you didn't do well on. If you were unsuccessful, this will help you prepare for a retake examination.

When you leave the testing room, the test administrator will give you a printed copy of the certification examination report. It will report your score and might have the breakdown of how you did in each section of the test. You should definitely hold on to this report. In the event that the testing center computer loses information about your test, this is your proof that you took the examination.

If you passed the examination, "Congratulations!" At the end of the testing day, the testing center's computer will connect to the testing company's computer and upload your test results. The WordPerfect Corporation Certification Department will then download the results to its computer. WordPerfect downloads test results Monday through Friday. In two to four weeks, you should receive a letter welcoming you to WordPerfect's Certified Partner Program. If you took the test during a beta period, official notification might take longer than four weeks.

If you didn't pass the examination, you should consider the test you just completed as preparation for passing the next examination. Use the result sheet and your key-point notations (made outside the testing center) to strengthen your weaknesses and achieve a passing score next time.

Remember the discounted examination fee for retakes. WordPerfect Corporation has no limitation on the number of re-examinations that a person can take.

Given the nature of the WordPerfect examinations—testing for expertise, not just competency—potentially many people will not pass the examination. A few suggestions can help you "turn a loss into a win" and pass the examination.

Retesting tips

If you were very close to passing, say within 10 points, please don't wait a week or two before going back and taking the examination again. You need to quickly review and get back in there in the next several days. Because you were that close, you should sit down with your student kit or the product manuals or talk to your instructor and figure out what topics proved difficult. The chances of you getting exactly the same examination again are slim, but you might be asked several of the same questions again.

If you were not that close, or if you felt that you were guessing at many of the answers, the key to passing the retake is to not feel sorry for yourself immediately after the examination is over. You need to go somewhere quiet and go over the examination in your mind. Get a piece of paper and write down information about questions that you were unsure of or had difficulty with; the sooner you do this, the better. Use the information on the score report to help determine the weak areas. Put simply: You have to go back and study what you didn't know. Write down anything that will help you prepare for the next test.

The most important point we can make about taking the examinations is *try not to be nervous*. People who are nervous make unnecessary mistakes that are usually recognized only after completing the examination. You studied and prepared diligently; carry that same attitude and methodology into the test session and don't rush through the certification examination.

Some people might only have access to a testing center one day per week. WordPerfect examinations are very rigorous, and you should only plan on taking one per day.

Finally, don't give up. Everyone who passes the examination is WordPerfect certified. Certificate holders are on a level playing field. No record is kept indicating how many times a test was taken.

Part 3

How to use your certification

Now that you are certified

CHAPTER 7

Congratulations!

Once you have received notification from WordPerfect Corporation's Certification Department that it has received your passing test score, you are officially certified. Now that you've passed the certification examination, you probably think the hardest part is behind you. In fact, many find the certification examination to be a challenge that provides an opportunity to learn about the unknown features of WordPerfect products. Your next challenge is using your certification to your best advantage.

You will find that there is no "right" way to use your certification. Many people, especially those who are not certified, will dismiss your certification as being nothing out of the ordinary.

This chapter contains our suggestions for preparation that every certified person should do after certification is achieved. We have included most of the tricks that we have learned over the past several years and tips that we learned talking with other certified partners while developing this book. We don't have a corner on the WordPerfect market, but these are some important ideas that you might want to take a look at.

We've broken this chapter down with information to include people at all stages of their careers and at different certification levels. The subsection "For all certified partners" is general information for everyone at all levels of certification. "Seeking employment or improving your current job" contains our suggestions for using certification for getting employment or advancement. If you are seeking self-employment, read the "Consulting" section. Finally, "Training" contains information specifically targeted at instructors.

Please note that the specific benefits that each certified partner receives depends upon his or her level of certification (CBC, CPC, CSE, CI). Specific benefits were discussed in chapter 2; selected benefits from chapter 2 are discussed here in more detail.

For all certified partners

Certification does not mean that the learning process ends here. No matter what level of certification you have achieved, it is important to keep current on WordPerfect products, information, and related issues. These techniques will help you maintain currency.

It's important that you develop your own continuing-support channel to keep learning about WordPerfect products and improving your skills. We suggest you consider the following:

- Read the WordPerfect magazines and newsletters.
- Network with other certified people.
- Attend WordPerfect conferences.
- Subscribe to CompuServe.

WordPerfect magazines and newsletters

WordPerfect Magazine and *WordPerfect for Windows Magazine* are publications of WordPerfect Corporation. All certified partners receive a monthly issue of the magazine that corresponds to the product they are certified on. Each magazine is a valuable source of information for the word processing products. If you are not certified, subscriptions are available.

The editorial formula consists of columns and feature articles. The columns cover such topics as new product information, product tips, and questions and answers. The product information section appears monthly and features new hardware or software products of general or specific interest to WordPerfect users. The tips column features specific helpful hints from magazine readers; this column can be very useful to pick up new uses or features of the product. If you've come up with a great tip or trick, you can share it with others. Tip contributors receive compensation if the idea is published.

The question-and-answer column addresses technical questions that readers submit. It covers anything from sorting, paper size, labels, and special characters, to printing problems with specific printers. Again, this is a great column for picking up tips and tricks. Reading about other user questions and the replies could save you hours of trying to figure out the problem yourself. The answers appear to be quick solutions, but significant research is devoted to finding the answers.

Articles in the magazines are very diverse for the audience. These magazines are intended for product users, whether they be novice or advanced. We found the articles on writing macros are very helpful. The magazines print the macro code, explain how the macro works, and demonstrate how or when it could be used. Numerous articles have also dealt with creating and using complex forms that could be easily modified to fit a variety of common business situations.

A nice touch is the "Final Keystrokes" (WordPerfect) and the "Out the Window" (WordPerfect for Windows) columns that appear on the last page of each monthly magazine. The columns are written by a new writer each month, usually on a whimsical topic not directly related to computers. They are intended to be light and fun, and we've found that they usually are.

Each magazine annually sponsors a contest that invites readers to submit their most creative application, whether a form, a macro, a merge, or whatever. *WordPerfect Magazine's* "Best Shot" Contest is always interesting, partially due to the creations chosen, and partially due to an extensive profile of the winner.

You may also purchase a disk of the month that is made available for each issue; a 12-month subscription for the disks is also available. The disks contain macros, styles, and forms that are featured in the monthly articles. Purchasing the disk will save you hours of keying in the code that is indicated in the articles.

You can get more information about *WordPerfect Magazine* and *WordPerfect for Windows* magazines by contacting WordPerfect magazines at the phone number listed in appendix B.

If you own a WordPerfect software product you might already be familiar with the *WordPerfect Report*, which is published quarterly by WordPerfect Corporation and is intended for licensed users of WordPerfect products. The *Report* is an update on software developments and events of interest to customers. It primarily contains marketing information about new and existing products, customer-support policy news, and a complete listing of the WordPerfect-support telephone numbers.

If you do not already receive *WordPerfect Report*, you may contact the publication at the phone number listed in appendix B.

A great source of WordPerfect product information is the *WordPerfect Reseller Report*. This newsletter is published monthly by WordPerfect Corporation and is distributed to all registered U.S. and Canadian resellers of WordPerfect Corporation software. It is a great reference because it keeps you up-to-date regarding which WordPerfect products are currently shipping and the release dates for upcoming products. It also lists all the system requirements for using the products.

Pricing and software packaging options are discussed in the newsletter. It's good to have firsthand knowledge from WordPerfect about how the products are going to be packaged. How much does it cost for additional licenses? Do the additional licenses come with documentation? It publishes information about buying software upgrades from WordPerfect Corporation and includes information about competitive trade-ups when switching from a competitor's application to the WordPerfect application.

The newsletter is valuable for information about special offers, such as additional software that is packaged with a third-party product from a different software vendor. It's good to know this in advance so that you can be prepared to use and train on the other product.

Reseller Report also contains timely information about free upgrade periods, which means if you bought a copy of the program between certain dates and a newer version is released within that time, you are able to get a free upgrade to the latest version. *Reseller Report* also shows some of the new features that will be available in the new

releases of the software. Interim releases that are being shipped also receive attention in the newsletter.

For more information about the *WordPerfect Reseller Report*, contact reseller feedback at the telephone number listed in appendix B.

In late 1993, WordPerfect Corporation started a specific WordPerfect Office newsletter: *WordPerfect Workgroup Expert*. The intended audience is people who install or maintain the Office or InForms products in a network environment. This newsletter contains regular columns addressing such topics as questions and answers, product news, common support questions, and a basics column for new users or administrators.

For more information about receiving the *WordPerfect Workgroup Expert* newsletter, contact the editor at the telephone number listed in appendix B.

Networking

If you can't attend the WordPerfect conferences (discussed in the next subsection of this chapter), it is a good idea to attend user-group meetings in your area. A great place to get information about user groups is a monthly publication called *The Computer Shopper*. Its editorial formula is geared toward *direct buyers* who are making purchasing decisions regarding computer equipment. One regular department in the magazine is dedicated to identifying user groups in a thorough listing that is broken down by state. For subscription information about *The Computer Shopper* call 1-800-274-6384 (see appendix B).

If there is no specific WordPerfect product user group in your area, you might want to consider starting one. A good place to start is by joining other computer clubs and attending the regular meetings, typically once a month. Ask around to locate a PC-compatible or Macintosh user group, depending upon which computer you use. Seek out other WordPerfect users within the user group. Perhaps a *special interest group*, typically referred to as a "sig," is already in place; if not, volunteer to start the sig within the established user group. If an overwhelming number of people express an interest in the sig, perhaps you should start a brand-new user group dedicated to WordPerfect.

WordPerfect Corporation conferences

Networking with other certified people is very beneficial, and one way to do so is by attending the WordPerfect Corporation Certification conferences. Everyone that attends a conference is there for the same reasons: gain more product knowledge, take hands-on classes, and network with other people who are certified.

Before you attend a conference, WordPerfect Corporation will send you a questionnaire to determine what information you would like to see presented at the conference. This is an excellent opportunity for you to talk to other certified people and learn about their advertising schemes, how they promote themselves, how they handle difficult students, and the like. A conference is also a great opportunity to meet WordPerfect Corporation employees.

CompuServe account

If you have a computer and a modem, you should consider obtaining a CompuServe account. The level and scope of WordPerfect information on CompuServe is unparalleled (see chapter 8).

New employment or improving current employment

Many people will be drawn to the WordPerfect certification program because it is something they already know. The WordPerfect products dominate the software marketplace as the best-selling word processing package available today. Many people will use the knowledge they have to pursue certification and return to the work

force, or certification might become part of their current job responsibilities.

We have addressed the following important issues for people who become certified and use that certification as part of their current job or to find a new job. Specifically we look at:

- Certification and your current job
- Using certification in a résumé
- Certification in an interview

Certification and your current job

If you decided to pursue one of the WordPerfect certificates on your time—paying for certification classes, self-study material, and test fees—you should let your employer know about the time and expenses involved. It will demonstrate how serious you are to prove proficiency on the product you became certified on. It will also demonstrate how motivated you are to excelling not only on the software products but within the organization.

Don't keep your certification a secret. It is important to let your supervisor know when you have become certified. It is also a good idea to make a photocopy of your WordPerfect certificate to be placed in your personnel file in the human resources department of your company. Attach a letter with your certificate stating the hours it took you to prepare with courseware or in classes. It is crucial that the letter explain why you chose to become certified; emphasize how the company will directly and indirectly benefit from your new knowledge.

Using certification in a résumé

In today's competitive job market, you need a special skill market that lets you stand out over other applicants. Use your certification credential to accent your level of expertise.

Linda Smith
Main Street
Port Jefferson, NY 11776
Home Phone: 666-555-4444

Certified Business Credential (CBC) for WordPerfect 6.0 for DOS, WordPerfect Corporation, June 1994

Experience
Administrative Assistant, Brook Printing, Inc. (June 1993–June 1994)

Created automated time sheet collection system for office staff using WordPerfect InForms. Worked closely with marketing department to produce flyers, brochures, and advertisements for newspapers. Made up slide presentations for technical seminars.

Secretary, F&M Electrical Contractors (August 1982–February 1985)

Handled all correspondences for the Assistant Vice President of Sales. Scheduled appointments and arranged all travel plans for employees. Transcription of minutes of meetings.

Education
Business Certificate, Bretts Business School, June 1992

Computer Courses:

Keyboarding

Introduction to Computers

WordPerfect Introduction

WordPerfect Advanced Skills

Introduction to Spreadsheet skills

Computer Hardware and Software:

IBM PC

WordPerfect 6.0

WordPerfect InForms

Accounting package

Make sure you include the date when you became certified, level of certification, and products certified on. Employers might not fully realize the significance of certification; therefore, it might be very worthwhile to include a brief overview of what certification entailed and explain the beneficial consequences.

For the person who has just acquired one of the WordPerfect certification credentials, it could be represented in many different ways on your résumé. There is no typical way to represent the certification status on your résumé. Use your creativity to properly represent your skills on paper.

All résumés are different. People have different backgrounds with more or less emphasis placed in different areas, such as education or work experience or both. Emphasize what you feel are your significant accomplishments, and list the relevant experience you have acquired.

Many books and resources are available to help anyone prepare a résumé. Our sample is not intended to show you a standard résumé format, but to present a generic résumé that lists the certification credential. The sample résumé is for someone who has acquired the CBC certification fairly recently. She worked for a couple of years, took a couple of years off, and returned to work. She is using her most recent work experience and new WordPerfect credential to further her career.

Certification in an interview

Be confident when you tell your prospective employer about your in-depth knowledge of the software application packages you know. Point out highlights of your résumé. Anyone can state that he or she knows the product thoroughly, but you have the certificate or certificates to prove that you passed a performance-based test on the product or products.

Explain what it entailed to become certified and the experience you had becoming certified. Tell them how you feel you could be an asset to their organization by them utilizing your expert knowledge of the products. If you are looking for a software-support position within the company, let them know what you are capable of performing. Items worth mentioning:

- ➢ Organize the office environment efficiently with the use of the WordPerfect product you are certified on.
- ➢ Train and assist other computer users.
- ➢ Customize applications to meet specific needs.
- ➢ Create work templates.

If you have CSE certification, stress the fact you have the ability to perform all the necessary network maintenance and support required to install and maintain WordPerfect products in a network environment. If you have the CI certification, state the additional requirements you had to fulfill besides just passing the examination.

Consulting

If you plan on using certification to establish or improve a consulting business, have we got some ideas for you! The most important tip we can give to consultants is to *keep moving*. There is plenty of business out there for you. Get started, and you'll find it.

Specific suggestions for consultants include:

- ➢ Obtain business cards
- ➢ Define services offered
- ➢ Create a brochure
- ➢ Advertise

➢ Contact WordPerfect sales representatives

➢ Network with other certified people

Business cards

When you are certified, obtain business cards and letterhead. One advantage of certification is permission to use the WordPerfect logo on related documents. The WordPerfect logo can be scanned into a graphic file for use in documents, which saves you some money versus having everything done at the printer. If you are working from your home, consider renting a post office box for the mailing address on all materials.

Define services offered

You need to decide what skills you want to market and where your interest is. This could cover the entire spectrum of software services from installation to office automation to working on special projects.

Ask yourself, "Do I want to specialize in a particular product that I became certified on? Is there a select clientele group that I want to target my services toward, such as medical or legal professions?" If you are like most consultants and certified people we spoke to, you will be willing to work with any person or organization that respects you and compensates you in a timely manner.

Brochure

You will need a brochure describing your services, which is a requirement for being a Certified Instructor. The brochures will be one marketing tool that can be widely distributed to potential customers.

Include your company name, address, telephone and facsimile numbers, and the all-important WordPerfect Logo. You may want to list any group discounts you provide. Any special typeface and design on the business card may be repeated on the brochure for continuity.

The brochure should be typeset by a professional printer, or you can make your own. Making your own is not as hard as it sounds. Paper companies produce paper exclusively for brochures. Many types are available. Some are two- or three-fold stock paper with designs on them. Some have pockets for business cards. Others are perforated to be used as a card for a Rolodex file.

If you have a laser printer, making brochures can be a breeze and a great learning experience because you will be doing page layout and desktop publishing with WordPerfect.

What do you put in the brochure?
If you are primarily going to be teaching courses, you should list the courses you teach with a basic description of each course. Do not go into too much detail about a class, such as listing all the product's features that you will cover. If the description sounds too technical, your prospective client might become intimidated.

Sometimes the best description is a generalization that tells the reader what he or she can expect to get out of the class. The description should list the prerequisites for taking the class, for instance "Basic keyboarding skills required" or "Introduction to WordPerfect 6.0 required."

It is best not to put course dates and prices in the brochure because they are constantly subject to change. Make a separate flyer or document with course dates and prices; describe the class schedule (dates, times, total class hours, etc.). Chances are your course content descriptions will not change as frequently, and if you should add a new course, you can always insert an addendum to your brochure. List any materials required for the course, and be sure to mention anything that you will supply, such as keyboard templates, handout material, reference cards, and the like.

If you specialize in a particular profession, be sure to mention that in the brochure. For example if you specialize in the legal profession, emphasize how the course can focus on features that are used in legal documents, such as table of contents, table of authorities, document headers and footers, and the like. If you are aware of a common task in legal offices—a utilizing form for setting up court

appearances—stress your ability to streamline that task with proper training of office personnel or by preparing the form yourself.

Advertising

Before advertising and marketing yourself, think about the targeted clientele—industries and corporations that utilize lots of computers. Major institutions are almost always computerized or in the process of computerizing. Banks, insurance companies, schools, government agencies, and medical offices are a great place to start.

It is always convenient if you have a contact person within an organization to get you in the door, but this is not always the case. Try to find out who is the employee that makes decisions about purchasing computer hardware and software. When that person is identified, contact him or her via telephone and try to arrange a meeting, or do a direct mailing.

If you advertise in local papers that are relatively inexpensive, you will reach two different types of clients. You will reach the novice who might want some instruction for home use of a personal computer; plan in advance whether you will make a house call or train at your site. The local advertisements will also reach small businesses that are just getting started.

You will also receive telephone calls from people just looking for free advice. We have found it best to give *some* advice over the telephone. If someone finds you personable and willing to help, when he or she is ready to actually set up an appointment, you will be remembered as the person who provided great advice and will most likely call for your services.

If your goal is corporate accounts or a select clientele, you might want to advertise in trade magazines or monthly newsletters that target those businesses.

WordPerfect Magazine is another place that you can advertise. You will be in an ad listed with other Certified Instructors.

Networking

You can find out about other WordPerfect Certified people by obtaining the *WordPerfect Corporation Training Directory*, which is updated the first of every month to include all new applicants that have met the requirements of the Certified Instructor program. It's good to know people who are certified in other states because sometimes companies that have regional offices are looking for training in all their locations.

If you are not able to travel to them all, you will be able to subcontract or work out a mutually beneficial relationship with another certified person. You will have faith in this person knowing that he or she has passed the requirements that you had to fulfill and have some insight as to the knowledge that he or she possesses.

Networking with other WordPerfect certified people is important, but networking with other types of certified people is also beneficial. You might want to consider joining up with someone who is Novell or Microsoft certified.

In the course of your consulting, you might have requests for applications out of your domain. You can still provide a service by recommending a certified trainer from within your network; contact the trainer, as well, to let him or her know about the potential client. It seems that when people think you know about computers, they assume you know about every possible program and piece of hardware. If you can hook up with another person or company that specializes in a different domain than yours, it can be mutually beneficial to both parties. Not only will it lead to more referrals, but you will be able to take on more jobs and subcontract out some work.

Contact a sales representative

One of the first things we suggest you do is find out the name of your region's WordPerfect sales representative; contact WordPerfect Corporation for the information. Call the rep and arrange a meeting where you can introduce yourself, explain your goals as a CI, and

emphasize your strengths. The rep doesn't have to talk to you, but the knowledge that a certified and motivated expert is available for recommendations to clients can't hurt.

Training

If you are going into the training business, supplement the consulting tips with:

- Low-cost software
- Telephone answering machine or service
- Student database
- Training documentation (that you develop)

Low-cost software (CI CSE CPC)

WordPerfect will sell certificate holders copies of any product as *permanent evaluation software*. You will receive updates as they become available. Note that *all* software products are available, not just the product(s) that you are certified for.

Telephone Answering Service/Machine

Make sure you have a telephone answering machine or telephone answering service when you begin your business. If working from your home, establish a separate phone line so it can be dedicated to your business.

Develop Client Database

Before you do anything else, immediately start a client database, if necessary on index cards rather than a computer program just to get the ball rolling. Record information about who your clients are and

what you are doing for them. This is required information for Certified Instructors and an important tool for support personnel and consultants.

In creating a database we recommend that the minimum information you include is client's name, courses taken, and telephone number. We have found it useful to include more. Specifically, we include name and address (for mailings), telephone number, class(es) taken, and comments such as if the client had a problem, a class was missed, or if we were called after the class for more information. We also try to track if a client refers us to anyone.

Always have students fill out a simple questionnaire or survey before they take a class with you. The table at the end of this chapter is an excellent sample survey.

The more you know about your students, the better you can assess their needs. By putting this information into a database, you will be able to query the data, perform searches, and create reports on information sorted by any variable. A good example of this would be determining all the people who took a particular class within the last 90 days to offer them an advanced class covering the next set of topics. You would be able to target just those users.

An intact database will keep all the information easily accessible if WordPerfect or a prospective client requests it. This information will be beneficial when you do client mailings.

Where do you find clients when you are new to the training industry?

If you are just starting out teaching, one way to begin building your client database is to teach adult education programs in your local school district. Adult education classes draw a large crowd because they are relatively inexpensive compared to college courses or local training centers. Even if the pay is not what you would anticipate, the exposure can be considered another form of advertising and marketing.

You are out there teaching, demonstrating your skills to students who will be impressed. A lot of times these students go back to their place

of business and tell others about the positive experience they had taking your class. Not only will word get around about your talent, but a former student might be the person you need to market yourself within an organization.

Libraries are also always welcoming opportunities for new programs at their facilities. When teaching in either an adult education program or library, you will find both environments to be very casual. You should be prepared for users with all different levels of experience. Do not overwhelm a novice; do not bore an advanced user. These classes will be filled with beginners who have never turned on a computer and super-users who are there just to pick up a couple of pointers. Always have some extra material prepared for the person who wants to go and work ahead independently. Let them know that the majority of the class is at a certain level and you would like to keep the class together, but you are willing to work with the individual when time permits.

Students that usually sign up for these classes are the best people for references. They leave the classes with enough knowledge and skills to use the program or, at the very least, they overcome their computer fears.

Special interest groups (noncomputer groups) that meet regularly are another source of contacts. Some local groups to look for are small business associations, the Chamber of Commerce, contractor meetings, and local clubs, such as amateur radio and other hobby groups. Don't overlook computer clubs and related sigs. Volunteer to be a speaker at one of the meetings; you might want to prepare a short demonstration or simply talk about the software product that you specialize in. Perhaps you could show some neat features about the program that they didn't know about, or just tell them some general advice.

Computer stores are another great resource for clients. You could work out a deal with them to let you sell your services through the store. You could try leaving your business cards for store customers looking for assistance. You could easily come to some type of agreement that you would send business to the store in return for referrals. You might even want to see if the store is willing to set up a

small training facility in the back of the shop where you could provide your services.

To build up client lists, you might want to consider a couple of volunteer hours with a not-for-profit organization to help set up equipment or software, subsequently working out an agreement for payments in the future.

Once you become a Certified Instructor, you want to start training without delay. WordPerfect requires that Certified Instructors provide 15–20 references on an annual basis for recertification. You cannot forge references. One false reference or two negative references will be the basis for disqualification from the program.

Creating documentation

The best way to train others is to give them documentation and notes of the materials you will be covering. We make our own course materials for the different classes we teach. Depending on the length of the course, the books are anywhere from 15–35 pages. The books incorporate example exercises and step-by-step instructions for the features we teach.

Although the initial time creating and setting up the books is time-consuming, it does pay off in the end. Do not become discouraged when several revisions of your course materials are required until you feel comfortable; the revisions are a positive sign that you are improving the course with the refinements.

When you create documentation, you should bind the books or use a heat seal, not just staples. Make sure your company name and phone number are on the books. You might want to consider professional printing and binding.

The advantages of training and giving out documentation are that you are more structured in your teaching and you never forget to cover certain features. The order in which you teach the topics is important. Students love the training material because they leave with the notes of everything that was covered in class. Students learning a

new program are always intimidated in the beginning. It's hard for a student to work on the computer, listen to your instructions, and take notes at the same time. If students are told that everything you cover is in the handout, they will pay more attention to actually doing the keystrokes on the computer instead of writing endless notes. Students can leave the training session and sit by themselves with the handout, following your instructions to practice the feature.

Another great idea is to give out floppy disks with files that have already been created for the students. If you are trying to teach about the automatic speller, thesaurus, and grammar checker, a prepared document will help students place emphasis on these features rather than trying to type in their own example. Make sure the disks have a diskette label with your company name and phone number. This is another form of advertising.

You should have documentation prepared for all the courses you currently teach and courses you anticipate teaching. You might not have a big demand for teaching macro programming, but you should have some course material prepared on this topic so you are not scrambling around at the last minute putting material together if you get a request.

Documentation should be prepared in a way that you are able to pull out particular sections and use them in other handouts. Sometimes you will prepare a customized class for a client who requests particular features. It's a real time-saver to just pull out only the sections you need from a master documentation file.

Copyright your materials

It is a good idea to copyright your materials. You have created these documents and spent many endless hours working on them. Copyrighting will protect you from other people reproducing and distributing your notes. It is a lot of paperwork to copyright your materials, but you can do it yourself without a lawyer. For more information on copyrighting materials, contact:

Register of Copyrights
Copyright Office
Library of Congress
Washington, D.C. 20559
202-479-0700

This chapter gives you some ideas as to where to market yourself, how to use your certification in your current job, and also how to market yourself as an independent consultant or trainer. You've seen some of the essential tools you will need, including brochures, business cards, and client databases. Make certification work for you. You put a lot of time into getting certified; now get the most out of it.

Student information questionnaire

Name

Address

Home phone number

Home fax number

Place of employment

Work phone number

Reason enrolled in class:

Personal use at home: Computer hardware/software

Do you own a PC and what type?

Do you own a printer and what type?

Software currently using?

Work environment: Computer hardware/software

Type of PC you use at your office?

Type of printer you use at your office?

Software packages currently using?

Class information: To be completed by instructor

Class taking:

Software version:

Attendance record:

Instructor:

Technical support

CHAPTER 8

Now that you have become certified, people will automatically expect that you are an expert on everything that has to do with WordPerfect products. You won't always have an answer for every WordPerfect question that arises, but knowing where to go for the answer is the key to becoming an expert. This chapter focuses on how to obtain technical support on WordPerfect Corporation products from the company and other parties.

Calling WordPerfect

For years, WordPerfect customer support has been available to anyone and is useful if you have a specific question on a problem. In early 1994, WordPerfect Corporation instituted new policies that requires customers to pay for support. There were several important reasons for this change in policy, but they are not related to certification and as such they are not discussed in this book.

It is our opinion that even given these new pay-for-support policies, WordPerfect Corporation offers perhaps the finest customer support services for a commercially available software product.

WordPerfect customer support is available Monday through Friday during the hours of 7 a.m. through 6 p.m. Mountain Time. As of this writing, WordPerfect customer telephone support is free to all registered users of the product for a period of 180 days, which is approximately 6 months from the time of purchase. See appendix B for more information about specific WordPerfect Corporation support telephone numbers.

We are sometimes asked "Is it OK to call customer support to get help when preparing for the exams?" The short answer is "No." Customer support is there to help people with actual *product usage* problems.

One important fact to keep in mind is that WordPerfect Corporation expects its certified partners to be able to solve simple problems without calling customer support. When certified partners call WordPerfect, they use a telephone number reserved for their use.

These calls are immediately "escalated" and routed to more experienced support personnel. An important fact to remember is that certified partners will be charged a fee for a call if the problem could have been resolved via the printed documentation, the INFOSHARE (fax-back) system, or the INFOBASE (CD-ROM support database). Simple message: Make sure you cannot resolve the problem yourself before calling.

You will need to have certain information available when calling WordPerfect Customer Support:

- ➢ License number for the WordPerfect program in use.
- ➢ Type of computer that you are working on, including the type of microprocessor, type of display, and disk drive.
- ➢ The version and release date of the WordPerfect product.
- ➢ Printer
  - • Make, model, and configuration of the printer.
  - • Printer driver version (most up-to-date installed).
  - • Laser printer's installed memory.

Here is a sample of what your information list might look like:

Product: (WordPerfect, Office, InForms, etc.)

License number: (From WordPerfect product certificate.)

WordPerfect product version: (4.2, 5.1, 5.2, 6.0, etc.)

Release date: (Check Help screen or Windows About ... window.)

Make/model of computer: (Gateway 386, Compaq 386 SX, 386 DX, 486, etc.)

Type/version of DOS: (MS-DOS 3.0, Compaq DOS 5.0, DR-DOS 6.0, etc.)

Type of display: (CGA, EGA, VGA, etc.)

Type/size of hard disk: (200 MB SCSI, 40 MB MFM, 60 MB IDE, etc.)

Make/model of printer: (HP Laserjet II, Canon model XXX, Epson model XXX, etc.)

It is particularly important that you know the manufacturer and version of the *disk operating system* (DOS) in use on the computer. Computer programs such as WordPerfect function slightly differently depending upon the underlying operating system. The three major manufacturers of DOS are Microsoft (MS-DOS), IBM (PC-DOS), and Novell/Digital Research (DR-DOS or Novell DOS). You can usually determine the version by typing VER at the DOS prompt. Some hardware manufacturers include a "personalized" version of DOS with their computers. Examples of these "personalized" DOS versions include Compaq and AST. Check the computer's documentation for compatibility information.

Before you call, make sure that you check the CONFIG.SYS and AUTOEXEC.BAT files to see what drivers or programs are being loaded into memory at startup. It is usually a good idea to print the AUTOEXEC and CONFIG files out. Test the computer, if possible, by trying to duplicate the problem without the drivers or programs in memory. For example, *comment out* the line in the AUTOEXEC that loads the DOSKEY TSR. (To "comment out" the line, type REM and a space as the first four characters of the DOSKEY TSR line.) The people at customer support will need this information in order to determine if there is a software conflict.

If possible, you should also write down the steps that you performed that made the problem arise. If you can't repeat the problem, then there is a good chance that the people at WordPerfect won't be able to either.

If you are at a client site, confirm the local telephone number (including area code) and verify availability of a fax machine and its telephone number. The more information you have available, the more assistance the customer support people can give you, and the response will be in a timely manner. Remember that your customer wants you to resolve problems as quickly as possible, so gathering this information before you call helps the client gain confidence that you are knowledgeable and well organized.

When you first contact WordPerfect Customer Support, be sure to get the name of the person who is helping you, and write down their first and last name. Remember, if you are using the certified-partner support telephone number, you are are talking to a higher-level support-staff person (more experienced) than a regular caller. Many calls are resolved during the first contact, but if you do need to call back, you'll know whom to ask for.

If customer support is not able to come up with a solution to your problem while you're on the telephone, you should ask them for the *call tracking number*. WordPerfect Customer Support logs all the calls it receives in a database. The call tracking number helps a support person look up a particular call in the database. When someone calls back and refers to a previous telephone call, the support representative pulls up a summary of the previous calls from the same customer regarding this problem. Tell a representative the tracking number from a previous call for instant recollection of your situation if it remains unresolved.

When customer support does come up with a solution to a problem, sometimes it involves sending new, updated software to the client. WordPerfect Corporation will ship what you need either via U.S. Postal Service or United Parcel Service. You should ask if there is a way to immediately download the needed files to the client site. Some update files are available on CompuServe (WordPerfect files forum), and others are available on the WordPerfect Corporation bulletin board system (BBS), which is listed in the telephone numbers in appendix B.

WordPerfect INFOSHARE

The WordPerfect INFOSHARE system is an information fax service available 24 hours a day, seven days a week, 52 weeks per year; it's *always* available. Information can be obtained from INFOSHARE via a fax machine (or fax modem) and a touch-tone telephone.

The information found on the INFOSHARE service can be broken down into three very broad categories:

- Technical update information about WordPerfect products.
- WordPerfect product information (including pricing and system requirements).
- WordPerfect corporate policy information.

INFOSHARE documents are also available for download from CompuServe and SpaceWorks (discussed later in this chapter).

WordPerfect customer support INFOBASE

The customer support INFOBASE is a CD-ROM software package that gives users access to a library of information regarding WordPerfect products. Originally developed for WordPerfect Corporation's internal use, this is the same software that is used by technical support staff when assisting users on the telephone.

The information includes product software change notices, feature tips, technical notes, troubleshooting tips, and other information used by WordPerfect Corporation Customer Support operators to answer customer questions and help him or her better use WordPerfect Corporation products.

INFOBASE is based upon the commercially available product Folio Views, from Folio Corporation of Provo, Utah. This same software is used by Novell to create the user help system that is included with each copy of Novell NetWare. Many new users are surprised to learn that this software runs from DOS and does not require Windows.

INFOBASE is made up of a specialized computer program called the *search engine* (also referred to as *Folio*) and a library of searchable documents called *infobases*. Please note that when we refer to the WordPerfect product, we are using the word INFOBASE (capital I), and when we refer to a particular document, we refer to an infobase (lowercase i). When you start up the INFOBASE program, you are presented with a menu of infobases to be searched. When you select a particular infobase from the Folio menu, it's as if you were opening a book. Each infobase opens to a menu screen that appears to be a book's table of contents.

An infobase can be read sequentially, one page after the next just like a book, or nonsequentially by jumping from topic to topic. Or you can search through an infobase (or infobases) for information about a particular topic. When reading an infobase sequentially, you can use the keyboard's arrow or page up and down keys to move through the document.

Many of the screens have highlighted topics. All topics have a red-colored chevron symbol (an upside down pyramid) next to them. If the user positions the cursor on a topic and presses enter, the search engine opens a new document and retrieves information about that topic.

INFOBASE is a *Hypertext* document, which is an important feature. Hypertext is a system of links embedded in the document that allow the reader to jump from topic to topic. If you want to move to the next link, you press the TAB key. If you want to go backward to the previous link, you press the SHIFT-TAB keys. This is a particularly important feature in technical documents in that it allows the writer to highlight a word and then point to another portion of the current document or even another document to give the reader more information about that word.

Besides basic cursor commands to move through an infobase, the user can also choose to use either the mouse or a series of pull-down menus; the menus will work with the mouse or keyboard. (The mouse driver must be loaded at the DOS prompt before the Folio program is loaded.)

The common way to locate information in the infobase is to search. Folio allows users to search for information two ways:

- Block a section of text and then search all infobases for that text.
- Enter words in the search menu and see how many times they occur in the current infobase.

The block-text search feature is useful for looking up additional references to information that you've already located in the infobase. Using the search menu works well when you want to look up a particular topic in an infobase.

Another important feature for support personnel is the ability to switch between Folio and another application by pressing a "switch" key. In Folio, if a user presses the CONTROL, left SHIFT, and F1 keys, he or she is prompted for the name of an application to load. That application is loaded into memory, and the user can switch between the application and Folio by pressing CONTROL, left SHIFT, and F1.

When you receive your first copy of the infobase, spend some time looking through the WordPerfect Corporation (often abbreviated "WPCorp") Tools infobase. This infobase contains information about terms and definitions used throughout the infobase product, as well as the *Customer Support Style Guide*.

The terms and definitions section of the style guide infobase defines terms that might be unfamiliar to all users. We found that this section was very well written and easy to understand, especially considering it covers terms related to everything from the basics of computers (such as BIOS) to vendor-specific local area networking products (such as File Server).

The WordPerfect style guide infobase describes in rather extensive detail how the infobase was constructed. It exactly defines what an "underlined" term is, as opposed to a "highlighted" term. It also contains very helpful information about how to search an infobase. This infobase details which words to use and avoid during searches.

The WordPerfect Corporation Customer Support INFOBASE product includes information on all current WordPerfect Corporation products for DOS, Windows, Macintosh, and Unix systems:

- WordPerfect
- Office
- InForms
- PlanPerfect

- DataPerfect
- Presentations
- Others (including Rhymer and fax software)

WordPerfect

By far, the largest portion of the INFOBASE CD-ROM is WordPerfect word processor information including manuals, feature memos, and software change notices. There are also troubleshooting memos for WordPerfect for NExT, WordPerfect for Unix, WordPerfect for Mac, WordPerfect 5.1 DOS, WordPerfect 5.2 Windows, WordPerfect 6.0 DOS, and WordPerfect 6.0 Windows. A separate infobase covers all the WordPerfect language modules.

Additionally, the infobase has manuals and technical notes for PlanPerfect, DataPerfect, WordPerfect Presentations, WordPerfect Works, Grammatik, and the Random House Webster's Electronic Dictionary and Thesaurus.

WordPerfect Office 4.0

The INFOBASE product includes all the WordPerfect Office/Novell GroupWise documentation that ships with the product, a total of 16 manuals (including Shell). In addition, there is a separate infobase containing feature memos, software change notices, and troubleshooting bulletins.

Feature memos provide detailed description of some of the various features of the WordPerfect Office/Novell GroupWise product. Software change notices list all of the problems addressed by a specifically dated upgrade or release of the WordPerfect Office/Novell GroupWise product.

We should note that the INFOBASE also contains all the documentation and troubleshooting information for Office 3.1, the previous version of the product.

 WordPerfect InForms

The InForms INFOBASE is structured a bit differently than WordPerfect Office/Novell GroupWise. Separate InForms infobases are InForms Designer and InForms Filler, and a third separate infobase contains feature memos, software change notices, and troubleshooting bulletins.

The Designer and Filler infobases are structured like the manuals and contain all the information from the manuals. The InForms feature memos, software change notices, and troubleshooting bulletins. A search is required to find information.

 INFOBASE tips

An important tip about actually using the information in the INFOBASE: In order to print or make notes based upon the various infobase files, we found it convenient to load the WordPerfect DOS Shell and use the screen feature. The runtime version of Folio Views, which is included with the INFOBASE product, includes a limited printing capability. The Shell program's screen-capture capability allow us to cut and paste at will.

Another tip: When setting up INFOBASE, use a system that's equipped with a color monitor. We tested the INFOBASE product on several machines and found that while it works, the product was not particularly well suited to a monochrome VGA display.

Information in the infobases is contributed by WordPerfect Corporation Customer Support operators, problem resolution specialists, testers, and developers. Of course, this information changes on a daily basis. In order to keep the INFOBASE user up-to-date, the fee for the INFOBASE includes updates for a period of one year. Updates to the INFOBASE are shipped monthly to each registered user.

Before purchasing the INFOBASE, you should note that there are specific hardware requirements for running the program. Of course,

you'll need a CD-ROM drive and DOS drivers so that the CD-ROM appears to your system as the next hard disk. The infobase search program is copied to the hard disk of your computer when you first use the INFOBASE. The exact amount of space that the program files take up on your hard disk varies from release to release, so you should contact WordPerfect Corporation for more information. To subscribe to the INFOBASE service, contact WordPerfect Subscription Services at the telephone number listed in appendix B.

WordPerfect Corporation conferences

Another means for obtaining technical information—when new products are coming out, technical information is crucial—is by attending WordPerfect Corporation conferences. WordPerfect Corporation regularly holds product-oriented conferences that are attended by corporate support professionals and trainers. Most conferences are held at WordPerfect corporate headquarters in Orem, Utah.

WordPerfect's conferences are usually related to a specific product, such as WordPerfect 6.0 for DOS. Benefits of tailoring the conferences to a particular product include access to personnel who are working on the product and a lot of product information that goes beyond manuals and telephone support. Conferences commonly feature panel discussions with the developers.

Before you attend the conference, WordPerfect Corporation will send you a questionnaire seeking what information you would like to see presented at the conference. It's important that you plan out what you want to see. It's also vitally important that you accurately answer the questions describing your level of experience with the product. It is a waste of your time and your money when you sit in a classroom listening to information that you don't understand.

Everyone that attends the conference is there for the same reasons: gain more product knowledge, obtain hands-on experience with new products, and network with other people who are certified. The

people that lead the training sessions are typically drawn from the training, beta test, development, and support staffs. The knowledge and insight are unparalleled. Don't be afraid to ask questions, lots of questions, while you are there.

A key feature of the WordPerfect conferences is the opportunity to work with prerelease versions of the software products. This is particularly valuable to consultants, trainers, and people in the support business because they have an opportunity to gauge the magnitude of changes in new products. We attended one of the prerelease WordPerfect for Windows conferences, and we were stunned by how different the product was as compared to the product that we were used to working with. But that experience gave us the knowledge that we needed to go home and adequately prepare our clients for the product.

Networking with other certified people is an important benefit of these conferences. Attendees can share information about how they advertise and market themselves, work with training materials they have developed or use, and how they handle difficult students.

We should note that WordPerfect conferences are rigorous events. Conference planners often include dinner and after-dinner activities. If you plan on doing any sightseeing, add several days to your itinerary for personal activities before or after the conference.

For more information about WordPerfect conferences, see the telephone number listed in appendix B.

CompuServe Information Services support forum

Two sources of WordPerfect information are available via the CompuServe online server:

- WordPerfect Corporation Customer Support forum (GO WORDPERFECT)
- WordPerfect users forum (GO WPUSERS)

The customer support forum allows users to directly download files from WordPerfect Corporation, and ask questions for corporate support personnel. The users forum is a great place to obtain information and solutions about your WordPerfect problems or questions. It's also a useful tool for finding out about add-on products, obtaining WordPerfect Corporation news, and chatting with people who do similar work.

CompuServe Information Services

CompuServe Information Services (CIS) is a dial-up, online information service. Many computer and noncomputer companies use CompuServe to market and support their products.

For most people in the United States, CompuServe maintains local telephone numbers for easy access. CompuServe is also readily available in many countries outside the United States. Contact CompuServe at the telephone number listed in appendix B for further information.

Before we go any further, let us say that access to CompuServe costs money. Before you can access CompuServe, you have to obtain a modem and attach it to your telephone line. A word of advice with respect to selecting a modem: The faster the modem, the faster your connection, and you won't have to wait as long for information to be transferred over the telephone line to your computer. CompuServe does charge a higher rate for faster data transmission.

CompuServe charges are billed directly to your credit card. Corporations can set up a corporate account with CompuServe; contact CompuServe at the telephone number listed in appendix B. Each CompuServe account also receives the monthly edition of *CompuServe Magazine*, a valuable source of information about the system. The amount of money that you spend on CompuServe will be based upon the data speed of the telephone connection, how often you call, and how long you are connected.

For more specific information about obtaining a CompuServe account, see appendix B for their telephone number. You can buy a

CompuServe connection kit at many computer stores. Before you buy the connection kit, check the modem documentation because many modems come with a CompuServe sign-up kit included.

Once a CompuServe account is established and utilized, most people find they don't know how they got along without it. Unfortunately, those same people find that their CompuServe bills are rather high. Remember, the connection charge is based upon how many minutes you are connected. (Pay attention to prompts that indicate whether you are in a standard billing area or a specialized area that costs extra.)

You save money when you can view information without actually being connected to the telephone line and the CompuServe computers. Several CompuServe-specific interface programs can reduce the connection time. You "tell" the program what data you want from CompuServe, and the program does the rest: logging in, downloading the information you requested, and logging off. One of the most popular programs is CIM, the CompuServe Information Manager that is available from CIS. We use the Windows version of this program, WINCIM. Other programs like these are available; *CompuServe Magazine* is the best place to obtain more information about the other interface programs.

These programs allow you read and access all the downloaded information offline at your leisure. You can even reply to messages or write new messages offline. When you are ready, you may either immediately reaccess CompuServe and upload your messages, or you can wait until your next access when the new material will be uploaded.

In order to obtain WordPerfect-specific information on CompuServe, you'll need to join each of the WordPerfect forums. (Remember, there are two different forums.) There is no additional cost for joining either of the WordPerfect forums; your name and CompuServe user identification are added to the list of people who belong.

The people who manage the forum are referred to as system operators or *SysOps*. SysOps might work for CompuServe,

WordPerfect Corporation, or other related companies. Most SysOps don't work for any of those companies; instead, they help manage the forum in return for free access time. SysOps manage the flow of messages and files and enforce the rules for the forum; therefore, you should listen to their suggestions and respect their requests.

The WordPerfect Customer Support forum

The WordPerfect Customer Support forum gives users read-only access to a variety of files containing information about WordPerfect Corporation and their products. The CompuServe command to access this forum is GO WORDPERFECT. You should note that you can download all the information displayed in this forum from the WordPerfect Files forum. Users can also access the other forums—WordPerfect Files and WordPerfect Users—from the WordPerfect forum.

The following is the main menu of the WordPerfect forum:

```
1 About the WordPerfect Forums
2 WPCorp Product Information
3 What's New at WPCorp
4 Customer Support Services
5 Other WPCorp Services
6 WPCorp Files Forum
7 WP Users Forum
```

"About the WordPerfect Forums" explains the structure of the forums to new users. This file and almost all the files in this forum can be downloaded to your computer from the WPFILES library. "WPCorp Product Information" is a series of documents that contain information about each of the products produced by WordPerfect Corporation, broken down by the computer and operating system that the program runs on. Recent corporate announcements are contained under "What's New at WPCorp." "Other WPCorp Services" addresses a variety of WordPerfect programs and services, such as the trainer directory, software donation, and beta test programs.

The last two options are the "WPCorp Files Forum" and the "WP Users Forum." Each choice exits the WordPerfect forum and starts the chosen forum.

WordPerfect Files forum

The WordPerfect Files forum is operated by WordPerfect Corporation so that users can download the latest update files, obtain information about WordPerfect Corporation, and acquire technical information about any WordPerfect Corporation product.

To access this forum directly, users type GO WPFILES. The WPFILES forum accepts questions in the form of messages from users that are answered by WordPerfect technical support personnel. The exchange of messages between users is discouraged in this forum. There is no means for users to post files in the WPFILES forum. The WPFILES forum supports all WordPerfect Corporation products.

WordPerfect Users forum

Something that might seem strange at first is the fact that the WordPerfect Users forum is not operated by WordPerfect Corporation. The WordPerfect Users forum is sponsored by The Support Group Incorporated, a private company separate from WordPerfect Corporation. All this means is that the statements and comments of the SysOps do not represent WordPerfect Corporation.

To directly access the WordPerfect Users forum, users type GO WPUSERS. The WordPerfect Users forum is organized into different message sections that segregate related questions and comments. There are message sections dedicated to different versions of WordPerfect word processing products (versions 5.X and 6.X), specific types of problems such as printing or networks, and other products, such as Office and Presentations. You can also contact people from *WordPerfect Magazine* and the corporate communications department.

Users can upload files to WPUSERS in order to share information with other users. Uploaded files are scanned for viruses and then added to the files section of the forum. Many different files on many different topics are available to download.

Up-to-date information about the overall contents of the message sections is available under the menu choice FORUM INFORMATION. You'll want to read and perhaps print that information out if you are new to the forum. It is not necessary to view FORUM INFORMATION each time you access the WPUSERS forum, but you should check it occasionally for updates.

The forum is divided into product- or feature-specific topic areas. When you access a particular topic, there are groups of messages related to one another by the title of the first user's message. Groups of related messages are referred to as *message threads*. The total number of messages in the thread is usually in parentheses next to the first title.

Many inexperienced CompuServe members don't understand that all of the *public messages* can be read by all CompuServe users. Even if a public message and reply were written by other CompuServe users that you do not know, you can read the messages because they are "public." A separate portion of CompuServe is dedicated to *private electronic mail* (GO EMAIL). An email message can be read only by the addressee.

This is a list of sections in the WPUSERS forum with subsequent summaries of the general type of information found in each message section:

```
 1 WordPerfect 6.0 DOS
 2 Print/Font/Fax 6.0
 3 Macros/Merges 6.0
 4 Other WPC DOS Apps
 5 WordPerfect Windows
 6 Print/Font/Fax WIN
 7 Macros/Merges WIN
 8 Office/Shell/Nets
 9 DataPerfect
10 Macintosh Apps
11 Other Platforms
12 3rd Party/Books/Mag
13 WPCorp News/Policy
```

```
14 WordPerfect 5.0/4.2
15 WordPerfect 5.1 DOS
16 Present'ns/Graphics
17 Forum [Comment]s
```

The first three sections of this forum are dedicated to the WordPerfect 6.0 for DOS product. Section 1 contains general product questions that are unrelated to printing, fonts, fax, macros, and merge. Section 2 is specifically dedicated to printing, font, and fax questions. Section 3 is very specific in that it deals with the macro and merge functions of the product. Most general questions are found in section 1. Look at sections 2 and 3 for very specific questions, as well as many good tips and tricks.

Section 4 contains information about other WordPerfect Corporation DOS products, such as the WordPerfect Rhymer, WordPerfect Works, and PlanPerfect.

Section numbers 5, 6, and 7 contain information about the latest version of WordPerfect for Windows. General questions about WordPerfect for Windows will be found in section 5. Sections 6 and 7 will be more specific and usually are a good place to look for valuable ideas and tips.

Section 8 addresses WordPerfect Office and Shell. Because both products are used extensively in networked computing environments, this section also collects all network-related questions for these products and others. This is the appropriate place to post any questions regarding a WordPerfect product used on a network.

DataPerfect, WordPerfect Corporation's database product, is the focus of section 9. The use and programming of that product are the frequent topics of this section.

Section 10 deals with Apple Macintosh-related products. WordPerfect offers a word processor and a version of Office for the Macintosh. Section 11 discusses WordPerfect products on other platforms such as Unix, OS/2, and NeXT.

Sections 12 and 13 don't address WordPerfect-specific software products, but instead are dedicated to third-party products, magazines, books, and WordPerfect Corporation news releases and policy statements. Besides information about add-on products for WordPerfect software, you will frequently find information related to the WordPerfect magazines in section 12. The magazine editors are regular contributors to this section of the forum. You'll also see message threads about WordPerfect's own technical and reseller newsletters. The WordPerfect Corporation news and policy section 13 is intended for announcements from WordPerfect Corporation.

Sections 14 and 15 address previous versions of WordPerfect. Many people are still using WordPerfect 5.0 and 5.1; questions about WordPerfect 4.2 still arise.

The focus of section 16 is WordPerfect Presentations, which is the presentation graphics package, and any WordPerfect product that is used for desktop publishing.

Perhaps the most popular section is 17, Forum [Comment]s. This section has nothing at all to do with a specific WordPerfect product. It is a community bulletin board that is usually dedicated to nontechnical issues facing the community of WordPerfect users (politics, religion, cooking recipes, etc.). This is also one place to ask general questions about CompuServe Information Service.

Please note that the forum titles change from time to time, especially when WordPerfect Corporation releases a new product. You may obtain an overview of all the current forums by looking at the message title under "Announcements from SysOp."

It is obvious from judging the titles of the various forum sections that there is a definite bias in the WPUSERS forum toward the word processing and graphics products. The support for Office and InForms is at best weak.

When you come upon a problem that you can't solve, you can post a message on one of the WordPerfect users forum message sections. Often the people who respond to your questions are either people who have had a similar problem or WordPerfect Corporation support personnel. WordPerfect support representatives use an account titled "WPC (WordPerfect Corporation) Problem Resolution (73760,2460)"

to monitor the forum. You can find out more about the CompuServe account that is used by WPC Problem Resolution by reading the FORUM INFORMATION file.

When you first access the forum, you'll probably spend most of your time reading public messages and replies from other users. This is very useful because you'll usually pick up valuable hints and tips that are based upon their trial-and-error time and efforts, not yours. Please return the favor and post a descriptive message when you have a tip or trick that will save someone else time and effort.

CompuServe forum tips and tricks

The following is a collection of tips and tricks about using CompuServe to obtain technical assistance. These hints should be considered when using either the WPFILES or the WPUSERS forum.

Before you log in for the first time, you should spend some time learning about your communications or CompuServe navigation software. Keep the manual for your communication software package, and make sure any quick-reference card is close at hand. If your communications package didn't come with a quick-reference card, make one up. Don't waste time and money trying to figure out what to do next while CompuServe's meter is running.

Before you go online, make sure you have some way to record names, user IDs, message numbers, and other information that you'll need as you are online. At least have paper and pencil handy during your online session so that you can make a note or two. A better idea is to use the log, capture, or save feature of the communication package to help keep track of this information. A log file or similar feature records everything that was displayed on the computer screen.

Several of the CompuServe-specific communications programs offer a valuable feature: the ability to download an entire message thread. This way you don't have to be logged in to read all the messages that were sent back and forth. This feature can dramatically reduce your CompuServe bill.

Before you post a message asking for help with a particular problem, check to see if anyone else has posted a message related to the same problem; if so, your solution might already be there; if not, but you found some information that came close, send a public message or private email to the other person or people with the same problem. Post a new public message if your problem is not addressed in any other message; the public message ensures that more users will see your topic, which increases the odds for a helpful reply.

When you want to add your comments to an ongoing discussion, use the REPLY function. This feature is built into the CompuServe messaging system. Remember to direct the reply to the person whom you want to read your message. If you don't make that specification, the reply function automatically sends your message to the person who wrote the last message you called up.

Another important tip is to *always write a subject line that immediately draws someone's attention to your problem*. Thousands of subjects appear each year; you want yours to stand out. For example, you need help using paragraph borders. Putting a message up with the title WORDPERFECT PROBLEM won't draw the interest of all the people you want to reach. Something like PARAGRAPH BORDERS will precisely identify what your problem is related to.

In order to keep your CompuServe connection time down, have all the information about your problem organized *before* you go online to post the message so that you'll be able to clearly relate the situation. Remember, this service is charged based upon the length of time you are connected. You will need to know the type of computer that you are working on, including the type of microprocessor, type of display, and disk drive. You will have to know the version and release date of WordPerfect product you are using. If you are having a printer-related problem, you should find out the make and model of the printer and determine which version of the printer driver is utilized in the software.

If you need help with a problem, post a single message in whatever forum section seems most appropriate to you. If you're not sure where to post your message, don't post multiple copies of the same message

in different forums. If the SysOps think your message belongs in a section different from the one you chose, one of them will move the message. Multiple messages are typically deleted by a sysop before anyone can reply. (SysOps must control the volume of messages to avoid confusion and congestion that slows access for all users.)

When posting a message, type the message as if you were writing a letter to a friend. Words spelled out in uppercase are the online version of shouting; therefore, be considerate and remember to use upper and lowercase.

With a little practice, you will soon learn how to compose messages offline when you are not connected. You might take a full hour composing a complicated question, editing and tweaking until it is just right. Posting the message would be done automatically in a matter of seconds by the CIS navigation software. Review the communications software documentation for specific guidance related to posting prepared messages.

After you have posted a message, log in within 48 to 72 hours for any replies that might have been posted. As new messages are posted in a forum (either WPFILES or WPUSERS), the older messages are "aged out" and deleted from the system. If you don't check back, the SysOps might try to send the message to you by EMAIL, but you'll miss out on messages in the thread that were not specifically addressed to you.

An alternative to logging in often is asking a sysop to "save to a file" the message thread that interests you. If the sysop agrees that the thread is interesting, he or she usually will comply and tell you where to find the file. Make sure that you tell the sysop via email when you have downloaded the file so he or she can dispose of it if you were the only interested party. Conversely, extremely worthwhile files might remain available to all forum members for an extended period of time.

If you have a question and you don't know who to ask, address the question to ALL. Any message addressed to ALL is considered a public message, and everyone will have the opportunity to read it and possibly respond. If you have a specific question for a sysop, such as the location of a file or advice about which section would be best for a question, address the query *SYSOP. Only the people who manage the forum read the *SYSOP messages.

While it is very important that you include information about the problem you're trying to solve, be careful about what information you post. For instance, never put your home telephone number in any public message. If you want to send your telephone number to someone, post it in a private email message. *Under no circumstances should you ever post a message that contains your CompuServe password.*

Do not be bashful when you want to add your thoughts to a thread. Many, many people who use CompuServe are *lurkers* who just dial in and read posted messages. If you have something to add, post a reply to one of the thread's messages. Remember to stay cool. Sometimes people become excited about what they read in a thread and send a very pointed, opinionated reply. This action is known as *flaming*. Try not to flame. Remember that everyone has an opinion.

It should go without saying that profanity is not tolerated. We're not talking about extolling the virtues of Microsoft Word. Messages containing profanity are usually quickly removed by the SysOps.

If you've ever wanted to suggest a change to a WordPerfect product, WordPerfect Corporation also maintains an enhancement request account on CompuServe that can be reached at WPC Enhancements (73447,754). Again, you can check the specific CompuServe account ID that is used by this group in FORUM INFORMATION.

Dozens of other forums are on CompuServe. As you grow more experienced using CompuServe, explore other forums on related topics: computer educators (GO DPTRAIN), graphics (GO GRAPHICS), or a networking vendor such as Novell (GO NOVELL).

⇨ Downloading files from CompuServe

WordPerfect Customer Support and the WordPerfect Users forums make files available to download. As a rule, before any file can be

downloaded by a user, it is checked by a sysop for content and also scanned for viruses.

It is a wise practice to obtain an antivirus or virus scanning program and use it on all files that pass through your computer. It not only protects all of your files, but also the computers of all the people you work for or with.

All files available from a CompuServe forum are found in the forum's library area. You can access a forum library from the forum's main menu.

Accessing the libraries requires two basic file search functions: BROWSE and DIRECTORY. The BROWSE function allows you to search a library or all libraries for files that have a user-selected word in the subject line. The DIRECTORY function displays the name, size, and creation date of each of the files in that library section.

Perhaps the most important file in any library is the index file, which usually contains the name and a short description of every file in the library. You find the library's index file by using the BROWSE command to search for files with the word INDEX in the subject.

The WordPerfect Files forum library

All files found in the WPFILES library come direct from WordPerfect Corporation. Users are not permitted to upload files to this library. Most of the files found in the WPFILES library are fixes and patches for WordPerfect products. Numerous printer driver files are here. In addition, you can download files containing news and press releases from WordPerfect Corporation.

The following is a list of all the sections found in the WordPerfect Corporation Files forum library's menu:

```
1 WP 5.1 for DOS
2 WP 5.x for Windows
3 WP 5.0 for DOS
4 Office/Gateways
5 Presentations/Draw
6 DataPerfect
```

```
 7 PlanPerfect
 8 Other WP Products
 9 WP Products - OS/2
10 WP Products - UNIX
11 WP Products - MAC
12 Printer Drivers 5.1
13 Printer Drivers 5.0
14 WPC News/Services
15 INFOSHARE
16 WP 6.0 for DOS
```

Section 8 (Other WordPerfect Products) contains files related to WordPerfect Works, Grammatik, Webster's Electronic Dictionary and Thesaurus, and WordPerfect for NeXT. The remainder of the section titles are self-explanatory. Remember that these section titles are updated without notice.

Don't confuse the INFOSHARE section with the INFOBASE product described earlier. The INFOSHARE section in the WPFILES library contains text files that are normally available via fax. In order to determine which of these files you want to download, you'll need the fax-back directory via the WordPerfect fax-back system (see appendix B for the telephone number of the fax-back system).

The WordPerfect Users forum library

The WordPerfect Users forum library is a great place to look for files that will enhance or expand your knowledge of WordPerfect products. Please note that this is not the place to be looking for updates or upgrades, which are found in the WPFILES forum.

The following is a list of all the sections found in the WordPerfect Users forum library's menu.

```
 1 WordPerfect 6.0 DOS
 2 Print/Font/Fax 6.0
 3 Macros/Merges 6.0
 4 Other WPC DOS Apps
 5 WordPerfect Windows
 6 Print/Font/Fax WIN
 7 Macros/Merges WIN
 8 Office/Shell/Nets
 9 DataPerfect
10 Macintosh Apps
11 Other Platforms
```

```
12 3rd Party/Books/Mag
13 WPCorp News/Policy
14 WordPerfect 5.0/4.2
15 WordPerfect 5.1 DOS
16 Present'ns/Graphics
17 Forum Info/Misc
```

The files found in each library section are directly related to a message or thread that was or can be found in the related message forum.

Most of the library sections contain articles, tutorials, and utility programs contributed by other members of the forum. Many of the message threads saved by the SysOps are in the library files.

Section 16 (Present'ns/Graphics) will be of special interest to most people because it contains graphics files that are compatible with WordPerfect presentations as well as the graphics format used in the word processing programs (WordPerfect 4.X through 5.X).

CompuServe library tips and tricks

Even though the point was discussed earlier, always scan each file that you download from CompuServe for viruses. We are not saying that the people at CompuServe are sloppy, or that they don't always check. They do a fantastic job. But downloading a single virus-contaminated file would impact your work and the work of others. You can never be too safe. (It's a good habit to get into because eventually you might log into noncommercial bulletin boards that do not scan files.)

Download a copy of the index file every 60 to 90 days. Even if you don't need a file, having a copy of the index handy when a customer needs a file is an invaluable reference.

Make a list of the files that you have already downloaded; note any application version number to verify currency if an upgrade is issued. You don't want to pay for the file twice. After you've downloaded a file, make a copy of the compressed version on a floppy disk. We try to keep all downloaded files on a series of floppy disks using the same filenames that appeared in the forum index file. This saves space on

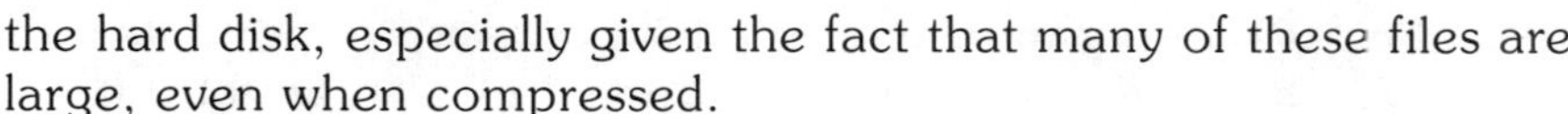

the hard disk, especially given the fact that many of these files are large, even when compressed.

Make sure that you are accessing CompuServe via the highest possible speed your equipment will support when downloading a file. A faster speed means less time to retrieve the file.

Other CompuServe forum services

Another interesting service available from the CompuServe WPFILES and WPUSERS forums is online interactive conferences. An online conference is an online chat session with a group of people. Whenever you type something on your computer, everyone in the conference can read it, and vice versa.

The SysOps post messages in advance telling all users about the upcoming conference. Conferences are usually center on a particular topic and feature a special guest, perhaps a software developer at WordPerfect Corporation or a member of the management staff. If you have an idea for an interesting conference topic that would be equally interesting to others, suggest the topic and a potential special guest by sending a message to the SysOps.

Other conferences can be arranged so that a group of people with related interests from around the country can meet and exchange ideas. If you want to hold your own conference, contact the SysOps.

CompuServe also provides electronic mail access to the Internet. In order to receive mail from an Internet host, people should direct a message to your CompuServe ID@COMPUSERVE.COM. For example the authors can be reached at the Internet address "73517,2007@COMPUSERVE.COM."

SpaceWorks

SpaceWorks entered the online-support marketplace in September 1992 as a dial-up support service that features a Windows interface

and WordPerfect Corporation-sponsored support. It's important to note that each time that we used SpaceWorks, no representatives from WordPerfect Corporation were available to answer questions online; answers came from other users of the service, not WordPerfect Corporation.

A major selling point of SpaceWorks is the fact that users can access the WordPerfect INFOBASE online. We found the instructions for using the INFOBASE feature to be very thin. This feature was very difficult to use, especially given that the SpaceWorks interface is different than the original INFOBASE interface. (Remember that Folio Views is a DOS program.)

There is no charge for accessing the WordPerfect specific information on SpaceWorks. Telephone numbers to access the SpaceWorks system are limited; we reached the service via a toll-free 800 number. Several other computer industry companies also offer support via SpaceWorks. The documentation states that Internet access is available.

Other online services

Several other online services are available throughout the United States and internationally. The most popular are Prodigy and America Online. Both services have WordPerfect-specific sigs, but none of the sigs are directly supported by WordPerfect Corporation personnel. Remember that any questions you ask are being answered by other users. This is not always a problem, but sometimes it takes longer for information about program changes to reach users on these services.

General suggestions

Support is a very important concern for anyone who has chosen to become certified on a WordPerfect product. The level of support that you will require depends upon how much work you do with each product. The following are some general suggestions for getting technical support for WordPerfect products.

Maintain a list of support telephone numbers. Check out the telephone number we have listed in appendix B and then add other support numbers when you need them.

You might want to develop a troubleshooting form fashioned after the list at the beginning of this chapter to list the hardware and software in use. This helps pull information together before you call WordPerfect seeking support, as discussed at the beginning of this chapter.

It definitely pays to obtain a modem and communication software. Figure out how it works; perhaps your networking has located someone else with WordPerfect credentials who would be willing to help you get everything set up. Whether you use CompuServe, SpaceWorks, Prodigy, America Online, or another service, eventually you'll have to be comfortable using a computer communication package and modem.

A CD-ROM drive would be a wise investment. WordPerfect is just one of several companies, including Novell and Microsoft, that provide support information on CD-ROM. WordPerfect discounts the INFOBASE subscription price to people who become certified. There is a learning curve when you first begin to work with a CD-ROM; the sooner you start, the better off you'll be.

What next?

CHAPTER 9

Hopefully this book has helped you decide if WordPerfect certification is for you. We've tried to describe products that are covered under the certification program and the types of certification that WordPerfect Corporation offers. We've attempted to explain why certification programs are offered and why becoming certified might help you in your business efforts. We've introduced you to people who are certified and tried to illustrate what certification has done for them.

Preparing for a certification examination is a challenging and time-consuming process. We've tried to show you how the certification examinations are developed and what the test objectives are so that you can make a decision about how to prepare.

When you become certified for one of the WordPerfect products, a number of other questions might cross your mind. One of the first is typically "When will I have to do this again?" You will have to recertify to maintain certification. Another question might be "What else can I become certified for?" Several other companies have certification programs. This chapter answers both questions.

Recertification: continuing certification requirements

Recertification will be necessary whenever the WordPerfect Corporation Certification Department mandates it. That might sound harsh, but it is true. It is necessary because the products change. As a rule of thumb, you should be prepared to recertify whenever WordPerfect releases a new major version of a product that you are certified on.

A major version is defined by a "dot zero" in the name, such as 5.0 (five dot zero) or 6.0. In the past, a person certified for WordPerfect 5.1 didn't have to worry about recertification until WordPerfect 6.0; however, if the changes to the product warrant it, the Certification Group at WordPerfect can call for everyone to recertify.

When recertification is necessary, it's generally a good idea to find out what the requirements are and get them out of the way as soon as possible. The Certification Group at WordPerfect Corporation will set a date by which you must be certified; alleviate personal stress by attempting recertification without delay, prior to the deadline. Plan on acquiring the new product, setting aside time to learn about new features, preparing for the test, and taking the test.

For example, even though one author (Brian) was very comfortable setting up and using WordPerfect Office in a LAN environment, it still took close to six weeks (studying 24 hours per week) to prepare for and pass the Office CSE examination. If you are consulting or training, preparation might take several weeks, and you should plan accordingly.

Certification on other WordPerfect products

As we discussed earlier, there are several levels of certification available from WordPerfect Corporation. After you have achieved the Certified Business Credential (CBC) certification, you might consider going for either CPC or CSE; however, be warned that you will have to pass the test for that program. In the previous WordPerfect program, all participants were "WordPerfect certified" even though their abilities were tested for primarily the WordPerfect word processing products only.

Becoming a Certified Instructor

Not everyone can become or should become a Certified Instructor. Besides the obvious requirement that you must pass either a CPC or CSE examination, not everyone has the necessary skills and personality to become an instructor. The process of becoming a Certified Instructor has been streamlined by requiring that all instructors pass the computer-based examination, but instructor

certification still requires that the candidate demonstrate the ability to instruct.

A popular misconception is that becoming an instructor is the next level after CPC or CSE. It most definitely is not. The primary benefits of becoming an instructor are only useful if you teach training courses on a regular basis.

If you are interested in becoming an instructor, you should seek to bolster your training credentials. The easiest place to start is trying to find a teacher preparation course at a local college or community education program. Some states require that adult education instructors take courses such as these. The courses are sometimes titled "Trainer Training" or "Teaching Adults." The courses usually concentrate on giving participants an introduction to the skills they will need to work with adults in a training environment. It is most definitely different from teaching children and very much worth the commitment of time.

⇨ Other certification programs

We included an entire section on other companies' certification programs for two reasons. First, you might want to expand the services you can offer a client or employer. It's been our experience that a potential customer is more likely to choose your services if you are familiar with other products, even if the potential customer does not want you to help with those products.

For example, if a potential client calls and asks for your consulting or training services for a WordPerfect project to be accomplished on a Novell local area network, it doesn't hurt to point out that you are also Novell certified.

Second, it helps you recognize that other certified people are out there for you to work with. Even if you don't choose to become certified on another vendor's products, knowledge of the certification program can help when you are seeking assistance.

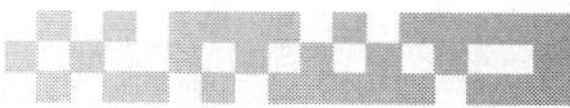

One word of caution regarding vendor certification programs. Before becoming involved with a program, you should determine if the certification that is earned is conferred on an individual or a company. Most certification programs call for the certification candidate to meet some defined requirements, and then certification is granted to the person. If that person leaves the company, certification goes with the person. Some certification programs call for the candidate and his or her company or organization to meet certain requirements, and then certification is granted for the company or organization. If the individual who took tests or met other requirements leaves the company, the certification stays with the company, and that person is no longer certified.

 Microsoft

Microsoft Corporation's certification program is the Microsoft Professional Program, offering certification on a variety of its operating systems (Windows, Windows NT, Windows for WorkGroups, and Microsoft LAN Manager) and end-user (Microsoft Word, Excel, Project, and Mail) products.

The Microsoft program also uses computer-based testing, but it requires that candidates pass a series of examinations before being certified. In most cases, candidates must pass two to three examinations within a six-month period to become certified. Candidates who successfully complete the requirements become "Microsoft Certified Professionals" for that product.

For more information about the program, contact Microsoft at 800-227-4679 in the United States, or 800-563-9048 in Canada.

 Novell

Novell Incorporated, offers certification programs targeted at administrators and service engineers for local area networking

software products. Novell's program defines four levels of certification:

- ➢ Certified NetWare Administrator (CNA)
- ➢ Certified NetWare Engineer (CNE)
- ➢ Enterprise Certified NetWare Engineer (ECNE)
- ➢ Certified NetWare Instructor (CNI)

The CNA program certifies individuals as to their qualifications for working with a particular version of the Novell network operating system. People who pursue and achieve this level of certification are generally network support and operations personnel. We found this level of certification would greatly complement WordPerfect CBC and CPC certification. CNA certification can be achieved for any operating system version by passing a single examination. CNA certification is available for NetWare operating system versions 2.2, 3.11, 3.12, and 4.0.

Certified NetWare Engineer certification is more advanced than CNA certification. Unlike CNA, CNE certification is not linked to a version of the NetWare operating system. CNEs are typically found in advanced operations, network integration and design (presales roles), and service/support positions. Novell CNE certification requires candidates to achieve 19 testing credits. Credits are earned by passing various Novell certification examinations; each examination is weighted and carries a fixed number of credits when passed. There are several "core" and "operating systems" requirements that all CNE candidates must achieve; generally speaking, CNE certification can be achieved by passing seven CNE-level examinations.

We found that CNE certification would be an asset to WordPerfect CSEs because both of those certification programs are geared toward network professionals.

The Novell Enterprise Certified NetWare Engineer (ECNE) program is an extension of the CNE program. An ECNE must accumulate an additional 10 testing credits. CNEs usually achieve this by adding specialty courses in areas such as internetworking NetWare and Unix or SNA environments to their existing CNE certification. Also, there

are additional specific operating and core requirements. For example, as of this writing, Novell requires all ECNEs to pass one of the basic NetWare 4.X product examinations. Persons interested in the WordPerfect/Novell GroupWise ECSE program might be interested in this level of certification.

The Novell CNI (Certified NetWare Instructor) program certifies those people who want to teach Novell's education courses at Novell Authorized Education Centers (NAECs) worldwide. The CNI program has very structured requirements that call for each instructor to attend (as a student) each of the courses that he or she would like to teach. All instructor candidates must pass a computer-based examination. CNI test scores are relative to scores achieved by other CNIs, which means that the passing score is usually higher (sometimes much higher) than the passing score for a CNA or CNE.

Like WordPerfect, Novell requires that instructor candidates have some training experience. Novell instructors are required to attend an instructor practical examination and teach a portion of a course for a Novell NetWare Technology Institute (NTI) instructor. The Novell instructor scores candidates based upon a variety of technical and nontechnical criteria.

Novell requires instructors to collect student evaluations at the end of each course. (Recall that WordPerfect Corporation has the same requirement.) The evaluations are reviewed by Novell. An instructor will be contacted by an NTI instructor if his or her evaluation scores fall below an acceptable level (as determined by NTI).

For more information about Novell certification programs, contact Novell at 800-233-3382.

Other companies

Other computer-training companies, such as Wave Training and Drake Training and Technologies (ComputerPrep), have certification programs. Some of these programs are specific to the courseware products sold by the company. (Recall that courseware is books and software that an instructor would use to conduct a training course.)

Because many of these companies sell course materials, being certified to train with their materials generally reduces the amount of preparation you need to do before visiting a client site.

Closing thoughts

As we stated in the introduction, if you decide that certification is something that you want, this book can help you become certified. We've presented what worked well for us when we sought certification. We've shared ideas and suggestions that can help you use certification to your best advantage. In closing, we wanted to take a moment to restate several of the most important ideas that we hope you discovered in this book.

Perhaps the most important idea is that many people might find the process of becoming certified very difficult. Certification is not something that can be achieved by just anyone. It is not our intent to scare potential candidates away from the program, but to give a brief and honest assessment of the level of difficulty. You probably realize that becoming certified requires hard work and the development of not just knowledge, but expertise with a software product.

A person can become certified at a variety of levels. There is absolutely nothing wrong with seeking and obtaining a Certified Business Credential (CBC) certification and then seeking the Certified Professional Credential (CPC). You will learn a lot about the product along the way and probably reduce the stress or tension level associated with preparing for the certification examinations.

When you become certified and you are thinking about ways of marketing your services, remember the reason that WordPerfect created and sustains its certification programs: to ensure the high quality and level of service that certified support and training companies offer to WordPerfect Corporation clients. Your certification helps make you part of this industry.

Part 4

Sample examinations

Sample questions

WordPerfect 6.0 DOS questions

Managing files

1. *You decide to create a shared directory on W:\APPS\WP60\FORMS for standard correspondence formats. What could cause the error message "Access denied" when you attempt to create this directory?*

1. You are in the wrong subdirectory when attempting to create this directory.
2. You have reached the maximum number of files allowed.
3. Another directory with this same name exists on a different drive.
4. You have an existing file in that directory named Forms.

2. *Valerie retrieves C:\BUSINESS\LETTERS\SMALL.BUS. What elements of the path statement are being used?*

1. The root directory
2. A directory
3. A subdirectory
4. A hard disk drive letter
5. A floppy disk drive letter
6. A network drive letter
7. A section name
8. A file name

Setting up WordPerfect

3. *Which of the following is NOT true about Display Pitch:*

1. Display Pitch specifies how many character columns will display on the editing screen.
2. The smaller the Display Pitch, the more spread out the text will appear.
3. Display Pitch formats indents, tabs, table margins, graphics box margins, and column margins.
4. The Display Pitch setting can be set anywhere in your document and affects the entire document.

4. *Your boss wants to hotkey between WordPerfect, Presentations, and DataPerfect. In order to maintain as much workspace as possible when moving between programs, where should you direct the swap files?*

1. To expanded memory
2. To extended memory
3. To the Upper Memory Block (UMB)
4. To conventional memory
5. To the High Memory Area (HMA)

Formatting documents

5. *Which of the following features can NOT be inserted in Document Initial Codes?*

1. Header A
2. Envelope
3. Center Page
4. Column Definition
5. Page Border

6. *When Autocode Placement is on, which of the following features will be placed at the beginning of the paragraph that contains the cursor?*

1. Center Page
2. Delay Codes
3. Header
4. Hyphenation Zone
5. Justification
6. Tab
7. Watermark

7. *Your cursor is positioned in a chapter heading of a school paper. If block is NOT active, which style type will format the heading correctly?*

1. Character Style
2. Line Style
3. Paragraph Style
4. Page Style
5. Open Style

8. *You have defined a Counter within a style that will number your questions. The style should also increment the counter before going onto the next question. Which of the following styles would allow you to Show the Off Codes and increment the counter?*

1. Paragraph Styles
2. Character Styles
3. Open Styles
4. Open System Styles

9. *You have selected a Paragraph Style to create a bibliography. The Enter Key Action can be used to:*

1. Insert a hard return.
2. Turn the style off.
3. Turn the style off and on.
4. Turn the style off and link to a Character Style.
5. Turn the style off and link to a Paragraph Style.
6. Turn the style off and link to an Open Style.
7. Turn the style off and link to a macro.

10. *The top margin for each of your documents is set at one inch, but they always print with a two-inch margin when you print to your dot-matrix printer. What formatting feature is designed to correct this automatic line feed problem?*

1. Advance
2. Adjust Text
3. Binding Offset
4. Top margin

Tables/spreadsheets

11. *Which of the following are true statements about floating cells? A floating cell:*

1. Is surrounded by table lines.
2. Is surrounded by codes.
3. Is used outside a table.
4. Is used inside a table.
5. Can perform calculations.
6. Can reference data from another floating cell.
7. Can reference data from a table.
8. Can reference data from a macro variable.

12. *If the table row height is set smaller than the font height:*

1. The font size will automatically be reduced to fit in that row.
2. The line of text will print over the table line.
3. The error message "Row size too small for font" will display.
4. The text will display below the table.

13. *Which of the following could Mark use to create a name for a range of cells?*

1. Variable_A
2. %Gross
3. SUM(A1:A10)
4. A10

Special features

14. *Which of the following Application Programming Interfaces (APIs) are supported by WordPerfect 6.0?*

1. TTY
2. CAS
3. FAXDIR
4. FAXBIOS
5. ANSI
6. CASMGR

15. *Which of the following programs identifies the modem/fax card port?*

1. FIXBIOS.COM
2. PTR.EXE
3. WPINFO.EXE
4. PORTUTIL.COM
5. FAXBIOS.COM

16. *You have a block of text in your document and have not decided if you want the text in italic or not. What can you do to the text so that you can come back and quickly italicize it?*

1. Create a Macro that blocks the text.
2. Create a BookMark that blocks the text.
3. QuickMark
4. Create a Hypertext link that blocks the text.

17. *While you were creating a report, you set three QuickMarks. You now need to reference material at the first QuickMark. Why are you UNABLE to return to the first QuickMark?*

1. Only one QuickMark is allowed in a document. The QuickMark last created is the only one referenced.
2. Only the first QuickMark in a document will be referenced. The other QuickMarks are ignored.
3. Prior to a search, each QuickMark must have the cursor before it. Only one QuickMark at a time can be searched for.
4. Each QuickMark must have a unique name assigned to it. The QuickMarks can be selected through search.

18. *To jump from a link to another place in your document, you need:*

1. At least two links.
2. At least one BookMark.
3. A Jump to Link button.
4. Any unique item in the document.

19. *In your document you have a Hypertext link that takes you from the beginning of your document to a BookMark. The option Run/Jump is grayed out when you enter the Hypertext dialog box. Why?*

1. The BookMark has been deleted from the document.
2. The HyperText link has been edited to run a macro.
3. The cursor is not on the Hypertext Begin code.
4. The cursor is not between the Hypertext link codes.

Printing

20. *You are attempting to print a document. In Control Printer, you receive the message "Printer not accepting data" and are prompted by the action statement, "Check cable, make sure printer is turned ON." The printer and the cable are set up correctly. Which of the following could be the problem?*

1. The printer port is not set up correctly in Edit Printer Setup dialog.
2. The printer driver has not been updated in the Select Printer dialog.
3. The printer driver has been modified in the PTR program.
4. The printer has not been initialized in the Print/Fax dialog.

21. *Kaitlyn only wants to see her Built-In and TrueType fonts when she selects fonts. Which of the following options will accomplish this?*

1. Deselect all graphics fonts except TrueType in the Select Cartridges/Fonts/Print Wheels dialog box.
2. Deselect all graphics fonts except TrueType in the Select Graphics Fonts dialog box.
3. Deselect all font types except TrueType in the Graphics Fonts Data Files dialog box.
4. Deselect all font types except TrueType in the Font Installer Select Font Type dialog box.

22. *Before printing your document, you change the following options in the Print/Fax dialog box: Text and Graphics quality to high and Number of Copies to three. How long will these settings remain active?*

1. The Output Options remain active for all documents until changed.
2. The Output Options remain active for the current session only.
3. Number of Copies are in effect until the document is closed.
4. The Document Settings remain active for the current document only.
5. The Document Settings remain active for all documents until changed.
6. Text and Graphics Quality are in effect for the current WP session only.

23. *You want to print 30 copies of a document that is 4 pages in length on a laser printer. You change Number of Copies to 30. Which of the following options when selected will collate in page order?*

1. Generated by Network in the Print/Fax dialog.
2. Generated by WordPerfect in the Print/Fax dialog.
3. Generated by Printer in the Print/Fax dialog.
4. Sort When Generated in the Print/Fax dialog.
5. Multiple Pages and set Number of Copies to 30.
6. Multiple Pages to Duplex and set Number of Copies to 15.

24. *Which of the following troubleshooting steps should be used to determine why a postscript printer is NOT responding to the print command?*

1. Type at a DOS prompt "copy con com1" enter "this is a test" enter "ctrl L" enter "ctrl Z" enter.
2. Verify that the correct postscript printer is selected in the select printer dialog box.
3. Initialize the printer within WordPerfect to ensure that the printer is ready to receive data.
4. At a DOS prompt copy the file Ehandler.ps to the printer and then print in WordPerfect to see if any error messages eject from the printer.
5. Check the port information on both the printer's menu and WordPerfect's Port dialog box to ensure that the settings match.
6. Set the wait timeout and job timeout to 30 seconds if a timeout error ejects from the printer.
7. Remove the paper tray to ensure that it is inserted properly in the printer.

Troubleshooting

25. *A student tells you the laser printer is not working. What would cause the laser printer NOT to respond to the print command?*

1. The printer is off line.
2. There isn't a Paper Size and Type code in the document.
3. The printer is out of paper.
4. The port isn't selected correctly.
5. The Location of the Paper Size and Type is set to Continuous.
6. The printer is unplugged.
7. The wrong printer is selected.
8. The directory for soft fonts and printer commands is incorrect.

26. *Which memory type(s) can WordPerfect use as workspace?*

1. Conventional memory
2. UMB memory
3. Extended memory
4. Expanded memory

Automating tasks

27. *Which of the following items CANNOT be added to a Button Bar?*

1. Table Create
2. Grammatik
3. Paragraph Style
4. Memo Macro
5. Layout Button Bar

28. *Which of the following WordPerfect 5.1 macro commands will NOT properly convert to the WordPerfect 6.0 macro language?*

1. {Search}Company{Search}
2. {Font}F{Down}{Down}S
3. {Graphics}LH{Exit}
4. {Block}{End}{Del}Y

29. *After merging, only the first record in your DATA file was merged. In order to correct the merge, you need to delete the:*

1. NEXTRECORD, at the end of your DATA file.
2. ENDRECORD, at the end of your FORM file.
3. FIELDNAMES, at the beginning of your FORM file.
4. PAGEOFF, at the beginning of your DATA file.

30. *A record is broken down into one or more pieces of information. Which merge command specifies the location of the information from the Data file?*

1. NEXT
2. ENDRECORD
3. ENDFIELD
4. FIELD
5. FIELDNAMES

31. *You need to create a merge that selects all the records that have the ZIP code 92703, and ZIP codes 92646 through 92649. The select statement should read:*

1. 92646:92649;92703.
2. 92646-92649;92703.
3. 92646;92649&92703.
4. 92646 :92649,92703.
5. 92646-92649&92703.

32. *When you attempt to sort a 1.5-meg file by postal ZIP code, last name, and first name, you receive a memory error. What are some possible steps you can take to be able to sort the file?*

1. Cut the file in half and then sort each half.
2. Remove any obsolete files off your hard drive.
3. Unload other programs currently in memory.
4. Use the /w=*,*,* start-up option.
5. Sort only by ZIP code.

Professional publications

33. *You have two documents. The first one contains a 6" wide table with the table position set to Left. The second one contains two columns, each 3" wide. If you retrieve the table file into the first column of the second file, what will happen?*

1. The table resizes to fit the column.
2. The table font size decreases to allow the table to fit.
3. The right side of the table disappears and does not print.
4. The table prints over the second column.

34. *An advertisement needs a graphic that must be faded so that text can be placed legibly over the top of it. This can be accomplished by setting:*

1. Contrast to 0.75.
2. Brightness to 0.75.
3. Increment to 75%.
4. Fill to Transparent.
5. Fill to White.

35. *You center a graphics box between the margins. Text will be added above and below this box. To have the box flow up and down the page with the text surrounding it, you must attach it to a:*

1. Fixed Page Position.
2. Paragraph.
3. Page.
4. Column.

36. *How can you add vertical lines between newspaper columns?*

1. Column borders
2. Table borders
3. Line Draw
4. Graphic lines

37. *After expanding a master document, you notice that codes that you had placed in your subdocuments are now gone. What has caused this?*

1. Auto Code Placement is on and has deleted redundant codes.
2. Codes will always be deleted from subdocuments if they do not have matching codes in the Master Document.
3. The subdocuments were not saved the last time the document was condensed.
4. There were too many initial codes in the subdocument.

38. *You would like the page numbering in your document to appear as "1", "2", "3", and the like. However, in your Table of Contents, you would like the page numbers to appear as "Page 1", "Page 2", "Page 3", and the like. How can you accomplish this?*

1. Change the page numbering format in the Page Numbering dialog to say Page [page #].
2. Change the page numbering format by placing a Page [page#] code in Document Initial Codes.
3. Change the page numbering format from the Define Table of Contents dialog to say Page [page #].
4. Change the page numbering by selecting the Page [page #] system style before generating the Table of Contents.

39. *Several items in the company report need to be cross-referenced. Which can be referenced?*

1. Paragraphs
2. Hypertext links
3. Outlines
4. Caption numbers
5. Footnotes
6. Comments
7. Volumes
8. Hidden Text
9. Chapters

40. *If you want to create a list for several types of graphics boxes contained in your document, you would define a list for:*

1. All types of graphics boxes.
2. Graphics boxes with captions.
3. Captions from several types of boxes in the same list.
4. Both captions and marked text in the same list.
5. Capitalizing the first letter of each entry.

Editing documents

41. *You are editing chapter 10 of your novel. Each chapter starts with page 1 and is a part of volume one. After selecting Go To, what should you enter to get to the first page of chapter 10?*

1. 1,10
2. 10,1
3. 1,1,10
4. 1,10,1
5. 10,10,1

42. *You select extended search to search for the phrase "As I lay sleeping". Extended search will look in which of the following items?*

1. Document Summary
2. Comments
3. Graphic Box Captions
4. Headers and Footers
5. Hidden Text
6. Hypertext

43. *When you press Reveal Codes on a BLANK document screen, you will find:*

1. [Open Style:InitialCodes]
2. [Open Style Initial Codes]
3. [Open Style:InitialCodes][Paper Sz/Typ]
4. [Open Style][Initial Codes]
5. [Open Style-Initial Codes-Paper Sz/Typ]

44. *After typing a document, you realize you need to change "ABCG" to "ABC Graphics." Which features will look for "ABCG" and substitute "ABC Graphics"?*

1. Glossary Macro
2. Go To
3. Replace
4. Search
5. Spell

45. *You accidentally added a misspelled word while spell checking an article. What dictionary must you edit in order to delete the misspelled word?*

1. Temporary
2. Document
3. Supplemental
4. Main

46. *In Grammatik, which of the following predefined Writing Styles will check documents at the highest formality level?*

1. Business Letter
2. Fiction
3. Report
4. Technical
5. Proposal
6. Documentation
7. Advertising
8. General

47. *You reviewed an article using Grammatik. The error messages are visible in the article when you return to WordPerfect. WHILE IN GRAMMATIK, you could have easily removed them by selecting:*

1. Options¦Unmark.
2. Checking¦Unmark.
3. Preferences¦Unmark.
4. File¦Unmark.

48. *You create a document that you want to use in place of the Gettysburg Address in Grammatik's Comparison Charts. What is the correct way to accomplish this?*

1. Enter the path and filename of the document you want to use in Customize Charts.
2. Retrieve the document, select Save preferences file, and replace the default comparison chart.
3. Retrieve the document and select the standard reference you wish to replace with the new data in Customize Charts.
4. Enter the document's path and filename under Save Statistics in a file.

49. *When comparing an edited document with a document on disk, which of these Redline methods can be used?*

1. Alternating odd and even pages
2. Alternating left and right
3. Alternating top and bottom
4. At the top of the page
5. At the bottom of the page
6. At the left margin
7. At the right margin
8. Printer dependent

50. *When you perform a Compare Document, where do the documents need to be?*

1. Both documents must be located on the hard drive in the default directory.
2. Both documents must be on consecutive document screens (e.g., Doc 1 and Doc 2).
3. One document must be on the screen, and the other must be on disk.
4. One document must be on a floppy disk, and the other must be in the default directory.

51. *Which statement about file Manager commands is not true?*

1. File Manager allows a user to search for files.
2. File Manager allows a user to print files.
3. File Manager allows a user to list files in the current and all subdirectories.
4. File Manager allows a user to create a new directory or subdirectory.

52. *Which is true about fonts?*

1. A user can supplement the built-in fonts with fonts from a cartridge or downloadable soft fonts.
2. Graphic fonts cannot be printed in landscape mode.
3. Font attributes can be modified to change the display of a font.
4. Graphic fonts can be printed in portrait mode.

53. *You accidently deleted a paragraph of text from page 12. The current cursor position is the top of page 1. Which feature cannot be used to restore the paragraph to its original location?*

1. Undo
2. Undelete
3. Paste
4. Copy

54. *Select the true statements regarding Watermarks.*

1. You can insert a file into a Watermark.
2. You can create Watermark B before Watermark A.
3. You can suppress a Watermark.
4. If you change the font in a Watermark, you must change the font back to the document font at the end of the Watermark text.

55. *Steven stopped his current print job and then restarted it later. At what page did his document resume printing?*

1. Printing continued from the point at which it was stopped.
2. Printing resumed from the beginning of the document.
3. Printing continued from the page following the last page that was printed.
4. Printing could not be resumed.

56. *Joe has a document that contains the following text.*

Apple
Banana
orange

After performing a sort (in ascending order), what would the order of these words be?

1. orange, Apple, Banana
2. Apple, orange, Banana
3. Apple, Banana, orange
4. Banana, Apple, orange

WordPerfect 6.0 for Windows questions

1. *In the Menu Bar Editor, you double-click on a feature to add it to the menu bar. Where on the menu bar does the feature appear?*

1. At the position on the pull-down menu where the insertion point is located.
2. At the end of the titles currently displayed on the main menu bar.
3. At the beginning of the titles currently displayed on the main menu bar.
4. At the bottom of the currently open pull-down menu.

2. *Which of the following Help features allows you to add comments to a Help topic?*

1. BookMark
2. Copy
3. Coach
4. Annotate
5. Tutorial

***3.** You would like to format your company letterhead so some of the letters in your company's title are closer together. Which typesetting option allows you to accomplish this?*

1. Letterspacing Justification Limits
2. Word/Letterspacing
3. Wordspacing Justification Limits
4. Manual Kerning
5. Automatic Kerning for Specific Letters

***4.** Which OLE option allows you to make changes to a graphic image in a graphics program and have those changes automatically updated to the image in WordPerfect?*

1. Insert Object
2. Paste
3. Paste Link
4. Copy
5. Cut

***5.** While creating a color palette, you want to blend some colors together, but the Blend button is grayed out. What are some possible reasons?*

1. You have the wrong palette size selected.
2. You have less than three color squares selected.
3. You have the colors displayed as a list.
4. You are using an invalid color model.
5. You are using the default color palette.

***6.** You inserted chapter numbers throughout your document; however, you notice that the chapter numbers are not increasing. What could be causing this?*

1. You did not manually increase the existing chapter number.
2. You selected Do Not Increment from the Page Numbering Options dialog box.
3. The Page Number Counter has not been set to Automatic.
4. The Page Number system style has been set to manual.

7. *You have numerous files created with a Courier 10cpi font. How can you print all the documents in Times New Roman without inserting a new font code in each document?*

1. Change the Printer Initial Font to Times New Roman.
2. Change the Printer Font for Courier to Times New Roman.
3. Change the Template Initial Font to Times New Roman.
4. Change Courier to Times New Roman using an Automatic Font Change.

8. *Which graphics box content types allow you to rotate box contents 90 degrees?*

1. Image
2. Text
3. Equation
4. Empty
5. OLE Object

9. *You create a chart using WP Chart and want to change the names that appear on the legend. How will you do this?*

1. Change the legend names in the Series Options dialog box.
2. Change the legend names in the Worksheet.
3. Change the legend names in the Format Legend dialog box.
4. Change the legend names in Chart Layout.

10. *After creating a keyboard in your new template, you exit and save the template. When you use the template, that keyboard is not the default. Why?*

1. You did not trigger the keyboard to open with the template.
2. You did not copy the keyboard to the template Initial Style.
3. You did not associate the keyboard with the main document window.
4. You did not save the keyboard to a .KBD file.

11. *You create a line style called MY LINE. In order to use MY LINE in every document you create, what must you do from the Graphics Style dialog box?*

1. Copy the line style to the default template.
2. Copy the line style to a style file.
3. Make sure that List Styles From Default Template is marked in Setup.
4. Make sure that Include Styles From Document is marked in Setup.

12. *Which of the following are true concerning Master Document?*

1. Subdocuments automatically update according to text editing changes made in the master document.
2. Subdocuments need to be condensed before editing changes take effect.
3. When saving a master document, it is necessary to condense subdocuments.
4. Master documents cannot be password protected.
5. When expanded, a subdocument is surrounded by [Subdoc Begin:] and [Subdoc End:] codes.
6. It is not necessary to expand or condense all subdocuments at the same time.

13. *You want to rename the DAILY directory to ARCHIVE. What is the fastest way to accomplish this?*

1. Select the DAILY directory, and then choose Copy Directory from the File Options drop-down box.
2. Create the ARCHIVE directory, and then move the files from the DAILY directory into it.
3. Select the DAILY directory, and then choose Rename from the File Options drop-down box.
4. Create the ARCHIVE directory, and then copy the DAILY directory to the new directory.

14. *(Refer to Fig. P4-1.) After performing a merge of 10 one-page letters, you notice that there is a blank page between each letter as shown in the figure. Which of the following options could correct the merge?*

1. Remove the NEXTRECORD command from the end of the Form file.
2. Remove the HPg code from the end of the Form file.
3. Remove the extra HPg codes from the end of the Data file.
4. Remove the NEXTRECORD command from the end of the Data file.
5. Remove any extra HRt codes from the end of the Data file.

Figure P4-1

15. *Which of the following Merge commands allow you to execute a macro within a Form file?*

1. EMBEDMACRO
2. INCLUDEMACRO
3. CALLMACRO
4. NESTMACRO
5. PLAYMACRO

16. *Which of the following are true concerning Help?*

1. You can create your own coaches.
2. You can print Help topics from within WordPerfect.
3. You can copy Help information to the clipboard and paste it into your document.
4. You can add information to an existing Help topic.
5. You can create your own tutorials.

17. *You are editing an automated template and need to delete the Personal Information prompt that inserts your name into the template. Which prompt will you remove?*

1. FIELD(Name)
2. <Name>
3. {Name\}
4. [Name]
5. KEYBOARD(Name)
6. MRGFIELD(Name)

18. *While in a table, you key the phone number 555-1212. When you move to a new cell, WordPerfect changes the number to –657. What can you do to prevent this from happening?*

1. Turn off Cell Formula Entry.
2. Close the Formula Bar.
3. Turn off Automatic Calculation Mode.
4. Change the cell number type to Text.
5. Activate Ignore Cell When Calculating.
6. Lock the cell.

19. *Which of the following are true about disk caching?*

1. Disk caching takes information from RAM and temporarily stores it on disk.
2. Disk caching takes information from disk and temporarily stores it in RAM.
3. Disk caching is a function of Windows.
4. Disk caching requires disk space to operate.
5. Disk caching requires RAM memory to operate.

20. *For software programs to access memory above 1024K, which of the following is required?*

1. A disk caching utility.
2. A memory enhancing utility.
3. A conventional memory manager.
4. A virtual memory manager.
5. A RAM swapping utility.
6. An extended memory manager.

21. *Which of the following steps ensures that you can fax documents from within WordPerfect?*

1. Select the WordPerfect fax driver.
2. Define the fax configuration in FAXWIN.INI.
3. Select the Windows-compatible fax program driver.
4. Define the fax configuration in WordPerfect.

22. *Although Row 1 in your table displays 2" high, pressing Enter moves the insertion point to the next cell in Row 1. What is causing this problem?*

1. Blank rows have been inserted, and the line style is set to None.
2. Row Height is set to Fixed at 2.0", and Single Line is selected.
3. Fixed Number Type is selected and only allows you to have one line of text per row.
4. Row Height is set to Auto at 2.0", and Single Line is selected.

23. *What are the differences between a standard and custom installation?*

1. A standard installation can use less disk space than a custom installation.
2. A standard installation installs only the essential files for program operation.
3. A custom installation installs only network workstation files.
4. A custom installation can use less disk space than a standard installation.
5. A standard installation is used to install to a network server.
6. A standard installation allows you to specify directory names for files.
7. A custom installation allows you to specify directory names for files.

24. *(Refer to Fig. P4-2.) You want the text within each paragraph of your document single-spaced and the distance between the paragraphs automatically double-spaced as shown in the figure. How will you do this?*

1. Create a paragraph style with two hard returns after the Style Off code.
2. Change the Paragraph Adjustment to 2.
3. Change the Spacing Between Paragraphs to 2.
4. Select Secondary Leading, and then specify 2.
5. Select Adjust Leading Between Paragraphs, and then specify 2.

Figure P4-2

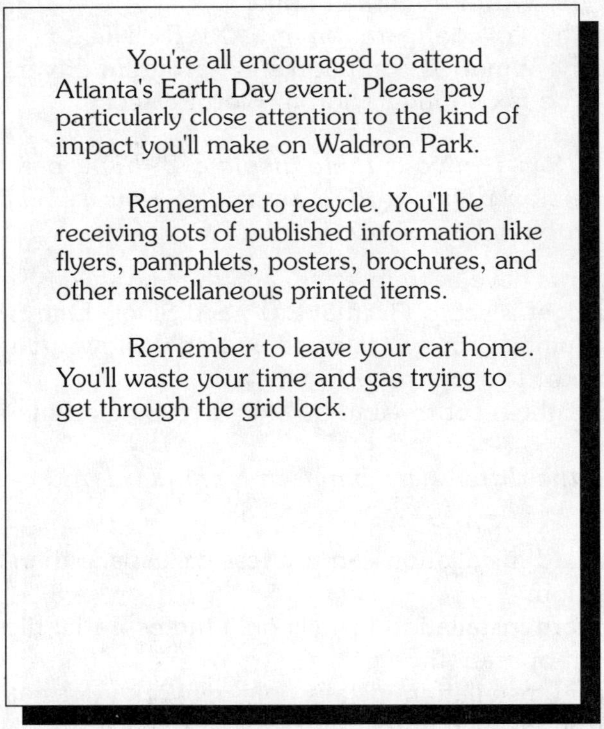

You're all encouraged to attend Atlanta's Earth Day event. Please pay particularly close attention to the kind of impact you'll make on Waldron Park.

Remember to recycle. You'll be receiving lots of published information like flyers, pamphlets, posters, brochures, and other miscellaneous printed items.

Remember to leave your car home. You'll waste your time and gas trying to get through the grid lock.

25. *While working on another computer, you notice that you can edit headers and footers in the document window. You would like to have this capability on your computer. What Display Preference would you change to do this?*

1. Mark View Headers & Footers.
2. Select Print Preview.
3. Mark Page as Default View.
4. Mark Show Document in Detail.
5. Select Full Page to be Default Zoom.

26. *You receive an ASCII Delimited file from a mail-order company and notice at the end of some lines there is a # sign. What do you need to do in the Import Preferences dialog box in order to remove this character when the file is imported?*

1. Mark Remove Record Delimiters.
2. Mark Remove Field Delimiters.
3. Mark Replace Record Delimiters with a Hard Return.
4. Insert a # character in the Encapsulated entry field.
5. Insert a # character in the Strip entry field.
6. Insert a # character in the Remove Character entry field.

27. *After creating a custom-envelope paper size, it does not display as a choice in the Envelope dialog box. What do you need to do to display the paper size in the Envelope dialog box?*

1. Set Paper Name to Envelope.
2. Set Paper Type to Envelope.
3. Set Paper Size to Envelope.
4. Set Paper Location to Envelope.
5. Set Orientation to Envelope.

28. *You are creating a Button Bar and want to add a Delay Codes button. How can you accomplish this?*

1. Select Delay Codes in the Button Bar Editor, and then select Customize Button.
2. Double-click Delay Codes in the Button Bar Editor feature list.
3. Drag Delay Codes from the Feature list in the Button Bar Editor to the Button Bar.
4. Double-click the Button Bar Editor button, and then select Delay Codes.
5. Select Delay Codes in the Button Bar Editor, and then select Add Button.

29. *(Refer to Fig. P4-3.) The dot leaders in Figure 1 appear too close together. What should you change to make them appear like the dot leaders in Figure 2?*

1. Increase the number in the Spaces Between Characters option from the Tab Set dialog box.
2. Edit the Bullet Style and place additional spaces between the bullets.
3. Edit the tab setting and place additional space between the dot leader tabs.
4. Create a Repeat Character that increases spacing between characters.
5. Increase the number in the Spaces Between Characters option from the Character Alignment dialog box.

Figure P4-3

Apples ....Page 25
FIGURE 1

Oranges . . . . Page 26
FIGURE 2

30. *You use Ctrl+End to move to the end of a document. On another computer, however, Ctrl+End deletes to the end of the line. Why?*

1. The computers are using different keyboard definitions.
2. The computers are using different Initial Codes Styles.
3. The computers are using different Insertion Point definitions.
4. The computers are using different keyboard models.

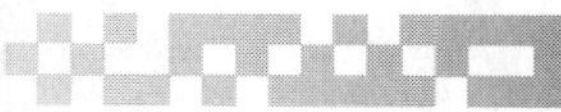

31. *When playing a macro you recorded, you notice it plays incorrectly. What should you do to fix it?*

1. Rerecord the macro.
2. Open the macro in a new document window and edit the commands.
3. Open the macro using Macro Edit and edit the commands.
4. Open the macro in Debug and correct the commands.
5. Run MCVWIN to correct the macro commands.
6. Reinitiate the MFWIN session to locate the macro commands that need to be changed.
7. Launch the Macro Command Interpreter to edit the macro.

32. *When do you need to manually save a macro?*

1. When you record a macro.
2. When you program a macro from a blank document window.
3. When you record macro commands to the Current Document.
4. When you record macro commands to a New Document.
5. When you record a macro to the Current Template.

33. *You would like a list of all WPWin 6.0 shipping macros. How will you accomplish this?*

1. Access the Online Macros Manual, and then select Shipping Macros.
2. Activate the Macro Editor, and then select Macros on Disk.
3. Open the Macro Bar, and then select Default Macros.
4. Select Print Macro List from the Open File dialog box.

34. *You want to use QuickFinder to find all files containing the word "WordPerfect." In which entry field will you key "WordPerfect" to accomplish this?*

1. File Pattern
2. Search For
3. Search In
4. Word Pattern
5. Options

35. *When you attach a graphics box to a page, what does WordPerfect use as horizontal reference points?*

1. Left Margin
2. Right Margin
3. Columns
4. Left Edge of Pager
5. Right Edge of Paper

36. *(Refer to Fig. P4-4.) When comparing the two tables in this figure, you will notice that the text in Table 2 rests on the rows lines and displays incorrectly. What would cause this problem?*

1. The first row is selected as a header row.
2. The No Cell Margins option is marked in the Table Format dialog box.
3. The bottom cell margins for the row are set to 0".
4. The row height is fixed too small for the selected font.
5. Table Leading for the row is set to 0".

Figure P4-4

Table 1		
Tables	1	2
Rows	10	15
Columns	5	10

Table 2		
Tables	1	2
Rows	10	15
Columns	5	10

37. *Select the true statements regarding Watermarks.*

1. You can insert a file into a Watermark.
2. You can create Watermark B before Watermark A.
3. You can suppress a Watermark.
4. If you change the font in a Watermark, you must change the font back to the document font at the end of the Watermark text.
5. You can have two Watermark A's in a document.
6. You can edit a Watermark image to make it darker or lighter.

38. *(Refer to Fig. P4-5.) What option should you choose to make the chart in Figure 1 look like the chart in Figure 2?*

1. Display Y2 Axis Labels
2. Display Data Labels
3. Stagger Labels
4. Stagger Titles
5. Data Legend Placement
6. Y2 Title Placement

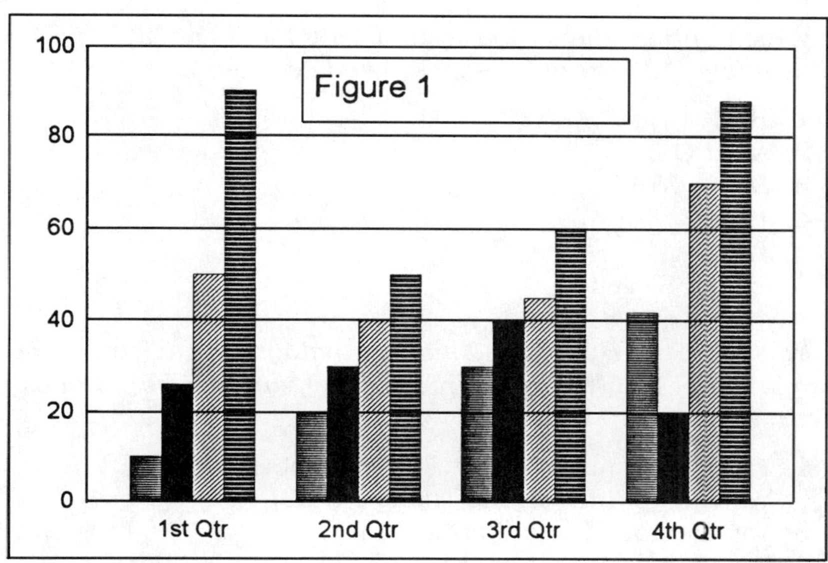

Figure P4-5

Figure P4-5

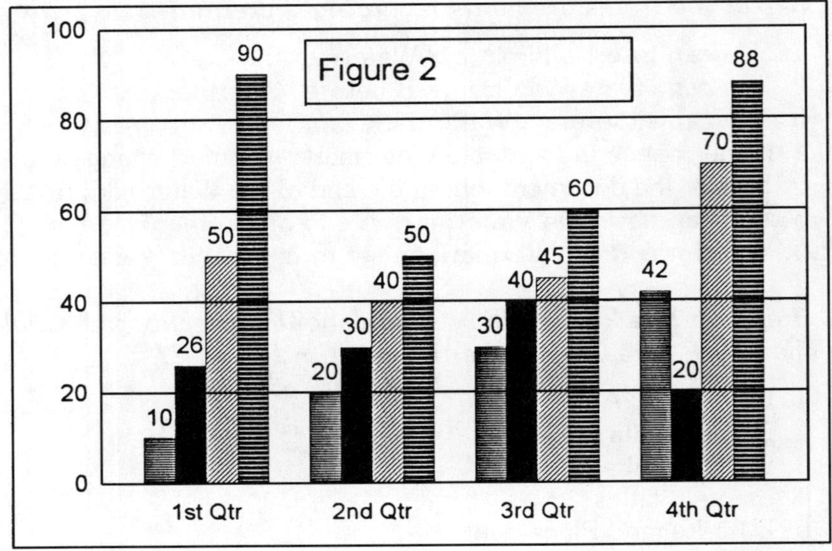

Continued.

39. *Which option allows you to find only the word "it," excluding such words as "itinerary," "transit," and "obituary."*

1. it!
2. Word Only
3. Whole Word
4. it*
5. it?
6. Extend Selection

40. *You open the Bullets & Numbers dialog box and select the Triangle bullet. But when you press Enter, another bullet does not appear. Why?*

1. You did not mark New Bullet or Number on ENTER.
2. You did not turn on the Triangle Bullet style.
3. You did not enter a Starting Value.
4. You did not press Ctrl+Shift+B after pressing Enter.
5. You did not set a Paragraph Level.

***41.** You create numerous styles in the current document. What can you do to use these styles in future documents?*

1. Mark the styles and save them as a separate style file.
2. Mark the styles and save them to the default template.
3. Copy the styles to the Personal Library.
4. Copy the styles to the Shared Library.
5. Save the user-created styles as a separate file.
6. Save the system styles as a separate file.

***42.** Which of the following startup options allow you to start WordPerfect without accessing the Personal Binary Initialization File and sets all of the Preferences to default?*

1. /sa
2. /n
3. /ni
4. /p
5. /pn
6. /x

***43.** While configuring a sound card, a fax card, and a video card, which steps ensure that they will function correctly with WordPerfect?*

1. Ensure that the CPU for each card is unique.
2. Share DMA channels between the sound card and fax card.
3. Ensure that each card has a unique IRQ setting.
4. Use a unique WordPerfect address for each card.
5. Keep the I/O address of all peripherals unique.
6. Configure each peripheral in WordPerfect File Preferences.

***44.** Which of the following are reasons why a sound clip would not play in WordPerfect?*

1. The sound clip is in WAV format.
2. The sound card settings are the same as another peripheral device.
3. The WordPerfect sound driver is not selected.
4. The sound card supports WAV format, and the clip is in MIDI format.
5. The Windows Sound Recorder is active.
6. The sound clips have been digitized and stored on the hard drive.

 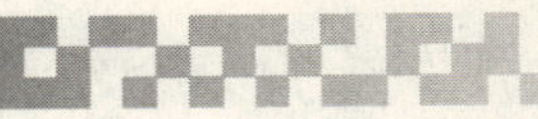

45. *Which commands should you use to create a conditional loop?*

1. SWITCH, CASEOF
2. ASSIGN, GETSTRING
3. WHILE, ENDWHILE
4. PROMPT, ENDPROMPT

46. *What are some reasons why you might be able to print a document from DOS, but not from Windows?*

1. The directory for the TEMP environment variable is invalid or does not exist.
2. There is not enough disk space to store the Windows temporary files.
3. You are using a serial port to connect to a network printer.
4. An incorrect font cartridge is selected.
5. The printer has insufficient memory.
6. The printer is not initialized for Windows.
7. The selected font is unavailable.

47. *While defining three parallel columns, you want to make the third column as wide as possible. Which settings could you adjust to accomplish this?*

1. Column Justification
2. Spacing Between Columns
3. Line Spacing Between Rows
4. Paragraph Margins
5. Column Widths

48. *You use numerous soft fonts when creating documents, but your printer does not have a lot of memory. How can you maintain the ability to use all of the soft fonts without depleting printer memory?*

1. Mark the soft fonts with a "+".
2. Mark the soft fonts with a "*".
3. Mark the soft fonts with a "+" and a "*".
4. Mark the Download Soft Fonts during Print Job option.
5. Mark the Download Soft Fonts to Printer on Startup option.
6. Mark the Present When Printer Initialized option.
7. Mark the Can be Swapped out when Printing option.

49. *Which of the following Table pull-down menu options will allow you to insert a formula into a cell?*

1. Cell Formula Entry
2. Formula Bar
3. Number Type
4. Format Formula
5. Formula Calculate

50. *You need to install a new printer driver. Which installation types allow you to install printer drivers without installing other files?*

1. Standard
2. Custom
3. Network
4. Minimum
5. Update

WordPerfect InForms questions

System administration

1. *Which of the following Query operators does not correctly match the corresponding operator symbol?*

1. (AND) ,
2. (WILD) *
3. (OR) :
4. (Less than or equal to) <=
5. (Greater than or equal to) >=

2. *You just queried your invoice database and found some unpaid invoices dated from over a year ago. You want your assistant to check on these invoices. How would you send the invoice information to your assistant?*

1. Create an .ML file from the Query screen including the Report information and mail it.
2. Create a .WPF file from the Query screen including the Report information and mail it.
3. Save the file from the Main screen in Filler and mail it.
4. Save the Report information as a database from the Query screen and mail it.

3. *To produce a report containing all of the loan applicants whose names begin with letters from M to R, which of the following conditions can be placed in the Name cell of the Query window?*

1. >=M<=R
2. >=M,<=R
3. >=M¦<=R
4. <=M>=D
5. <=M,>=D

4. *Which of the four links listed below is used as the default link in Query?*

1. The Primary Update Link
2. The Secondary Update Link
3. The Primary Lookup Link
4. The Secondary Lookup Link

5. *Which of the following is a requirement before creating a Join in Query?*

1. A Form Object linked to both databases.
2. Common data in Joined Fields.
3. Identical Field names in both databases.
4. An @JOIN calculation in the form.

6. *A time sheet form created using WordPerfect InForms needs a calculation assigned to an Entry Field that automatically calculates the sum of the weekly fields as soon as the values are entered. Which InForms calculation type will perform this operation this properly?*

1. Action
2. Change
3. Entry
4. Exit
5. Close

7. *Why would the "Save As Locked" feature be used in WordPerfect InForms?*

1. To determine if the form has been edited.
2. To store the form in the Security Database.
3. To prevent the form from being edited.
4. To prevent the form from being deleted off the network.

8. *On the Employment Application, you have used an Entry Field to allow the user to enter a phone number. What would be the Custom Data Format for a phone number so users could only enter numbers?*

1. ([X][X][X])[X][X][X]-[X][X][X][X]
2. ([A][A][A])[A][A][A]-[A][A][A][A]
3. ([N][N][N])[N][N][N]-[N][N][N][N]
4. ([#][#][#])[#][#][#]-[#][#][#][#]

9. *When designing the Employment Application, you locked the tab order of the applicant's name, address, city, state, and postal code fields. Which of the following statements are true concerning Objects grouped with a locked Tab Order when completing the form in Filler?*

1. The user will be required to enter input in each Object of the locked group.
2. The user will be required to move through the locked group in a certain order.
3. When the user attempts to move focus out of sequence, the cursor returns to the next Object in the sequence.
4. The user can use Tab to move to the next Object when the previous Object is blank.
5. The user can use the mouse to move to the next Object when the previous Object is blank.

10. *Which of the following "Auto-Increment On" methods ensures that each value is used in consecutive order?*

1. New
2. Consecutive
3. Successive
4. Add

Standalone systems

11. *Shared codes from which of the following WordPerfect products are compatible with WordPerfect InForms?*

1. WordPerfect Presentations 2.0 Win
2. WPWin 5.2
3. WordPerfect Office 4.0
4. WordPerfect 6.0 DOS

12. *Which of the following hold the WordPerfect license number for Designer, Filler, and Security .EXE files?*

1. WPFD.INI
2. WPFF.INI
3. WPFS.INI
4. WPC.INI
5. WPFM.INI
6. WPDF.INI

13. *What is the default location of files for Database Files after running the WordPerfect InForms Standard installation program?*

1. c:\informs\database
2. c:\informs
3. c:\informs\forms
4. c:\informs\learn
5. c:\informs\data
6. c:\windows

14. *Which of the following files are used specifically to run WordPerfect InForms Filler?*

1. FFWIN.EXE
2. FDWIN.EXE
3. FFQELIB.DLL
4. WPFFUS.DLL
5. WP{FF}.FFD

15. *When using the InForms Designer package installation disks, what would you need to do to install only the Filler application on a Standalone computer?*

1. Choose the Filler option in the Select Files screen.
2. Install the entire program and delete files not related to Filler.
3. Run the FINSTALL.EXE program.
4. You must have the entire program installed to run Filler.

16. *When doing a Standard installation on a nonnetworked computer, the Shared Code files are installed to which directory?*

1. C:\WPC
2. C:\WPSHARE
3. C:\WINDOWS
4. C:\WINDOWS\SYSTEM

Network systems

17. *Which of the following e-mail packages are directly supported in WordPerfect InForms?*

1. Banyan Mail
2. cc:Mail 1.1
3. Microsoft Mail 3.0
4. DaVinci Mail
5. Windows for Workgroups Mail
6. WordPerfect Office 4.0
7. MHS Mail
8. WP Office 3.1

18. *Which of the following are true about the location of Shared Code files for WordPerfect InForms given a network installation?*

1. They must be installed in the same directory as Designer.
2. They must be installed in each user's personal directory.
3. They must be installed to the file server.
4. They must be accessible to all WordPerfect InForms users.
5. They can be installed on the local hard drive.

19. *Which of the following conditions will prevent a user from signing a Signature Field in a form?*

1. User has no access privileges to the Security Database.
2. The form was mailed as a .WPF file.
3. User is not listed in a linked approval group.
4. The form was mailed as an .ML file.
5. User only has Read and Write access privileges to the Security Database.

20. *What options are available during a Custom installation that are not available during a Standard installation?*

1. Choosing specific files to install.
2. Installing Security separately.
3. Selecting directory names.
4. Creating specific directories.
5. Changing the display type.

21. *Which of the following startup options eliminate an "Access Denied" error when trying to launch Designer?*

1. /d-
2. /wpc-
3. /ne
4. /x
5. /nt-

22. *How can users retrieve, fill out, and return forms to their supervisor?*

1. The users retrieve, fill out, and return a .WPF file mailed to them by their supervisor.
2. The users retrieve, fill out, and return an .ML file mailed to them by their supervisor.
3. The .WPF file can be saved to a floppy disk, sent to the users who fill in the form, and returned to their supervisor.
4. The .ML file can be saved to a floppy disk, sent to the users who fill in the form, and returned to their supervisor.

Managing security

23. *What is the purpose of Security when used with a form?*

1. To determine if protected data has been tampered with.
2. To prevent protected data from being altered in Filler.
3. To prevent users from editing the form in Designer.
4. To allow you to input a network ID stamp on the form.

24. *A user with the appropriate approval privileges signs a Signature Field in Filler. At what point does the record become protected for authentication?*

1. When the record is added to the database.
2. When the password matches what is in the Security Database.
3. When the password and user ID match what is in the Security Database.
4. When the user ID matches what is in the Security Database.

25. *How is a Security Database set up so the department manager is the only one who can sign expense report forms?*

1. Assign the manager's name as the default on the Signature Field.
2. Assign the manager to the highest Approval Group.
3. Assign the manager to an Approval Group with only one member.
4. Assign the manager to the Manager Approval Group with the highest Privilege Level.

26. *To save time when creating a Security Database, you may specify the User's network ID as the default password until each user changes it. Where do you specify this option?*

1. Default Password Option in the Add User screen
2. Default Password Option in Designer Preferences
3. Default Password Option under Security Preferences
4. Default Password Option under the Admin menu

27. *What can the Security Administrator do if several users have forgotten their passwords?*

1. Look up the passwords in the Security Database.
2. Delete the users and recreate them in Security Database.
3. Create new users and copy everything except the password from the old user file.
4. Modify the users and change the password to their network name.

28. *A reorganization has occurred at your company and one department has been shut down. How can you delete the entire Department from the Security database?*

1. Highlight the Department in Edit User Record and press your Delete key.
2. Highlight the department in Edit User Record and choose Clear.
3. Choose View ¦ Department, highlight the department then choose Edit ¦ Clear.
4. Choose View ¦ Department, highlight the department then choose Edit ¦ Delete.

WordPerfect Office 4.0 questions

Single-domain systems

1. *Under which of the following conditions would a message server not be necessary?*

1. Two or more post offices on the same file server.
2. Two file servers, each with its own post office and a direct link to the same domain.
3. All users belong to a single post office.
4. All of the post offices in the system connected through an Async gateway.

2. *What are the minimum network access privileges that DOS/WINDOWS users must have in order to successfully run WordPerfect Office 4.0?*

1. Full privileges in both the domain directory structure and post office directory structure.
2. Full privileges to the entire post office directory structure.
3. Full privileges to the message server and post office directory structures.
4. Read privilege to the post office directory, and read, write, erase, and create access to the post office subdirectories.
5. Read and write privileges in the domain directory and read, write, erase, and create access to the post office subdirectories.
6. Read privilege to the domain directory structure, and full privileges to the post office directory structure.

3. *If you anticipate a large amount of message traffic between users on different post offices, which of the following options would improve the message delivery time?*

1. Run OFS for DOS on a dedicated machine for each post office.
2. Run the message server and OFS from a RAM drive.
3. Install more RAM on the message server machine.
4. Install a separate message server at each post office.
5. Run OFS for OS/2 separately for each post office on a single OS/2 machine.

4. *After completely installing WordPerfect Office 4.0 and configuring the message server, you found that users can only send mail within their local post office and not to any of the other post offices within the system. What could cause this to happen?*

1. Correct drive mappings have not been established for the message server.
2. OFS.EXE is not running on a dedicated machine.
3. Users have insufficient security rights to the post office directory structure.
4. Correct drive mappings have not been established for the users to the other post offices.
5. The message delivery has been set to Server Never.
6. The message server has never been started.

5. *When the Message Server information file (the CSI file) is created by AD.EXE, in which directory is it created? (Note: Your domain directory is J:\HOSPITAL and your post office directory is J:\HOSPITAL\ADMIN.)*

1. J:\Hospital
2. J:\Hospital\Cslocal
3. J:\Hospital\Admin
4. J:\Hospital\Admin\Wpcs
5. J:\Hospital\Wpcs
6. J:\Hospital\Cslocal\Css

6. *A user is complaining that she is unable to change the location of her archive files while other users on her post office are able to. What would be the cause?*

1. The user does not have modify rights within the \OFMSG directory.
2. The Archive Directory in the client Location of Files screen is displaying a "U".
3. The user does not have modify rights within the \OFUSER directory.
4. The Archive Directory in the Administration Location of Files screen is displaying a "U".
5. The Archive Directory in the client Location of Files screen is displaying an "L".

7. *How would the administrator force a user's archived messages to be saved to C:\ on the user's own hard drive?*

1. Send the user a message describing how to set Location of Files in OF.EXE Setup ¦ Archive Directory to C:\.
2. Restrict the user's rights to the WordPerfect Office 4.0 post office directory to read only.
3. Allow the user to only have access to WordPerfect Office Remote 4.0.
4. Set the post office Archive Directory field to C:\ and lock the user's post office with a "P" in the Office 4.0 Options screen in AD.EXE.

5. Set the user's Archive Directory field to C:\ and lock the user's account with a "U" in the Office 4.0 Options screen in AD.EXE.

8. *The WordPerfect Office 4.0 application off loads messages to the message server when the Threshold option found under Environment in Office 4.0 Options is set to Use App Thresholds and, _______________.*

1. The total number of affected mailboxes (sender's plus recipients') is less than the threshold.
2. The total number of affected user databases (sender's plus recipients') is greater than the threshold.
3. The total number of affected databases (sender's plus recipients') exceeds the threshold set by the user.

9. *Your domain directory is J:\HOSPITAL and your post office directory is J:\HOSPITAL\RADIOLGY. In which of the following directories is the Office userid.fil file placed upon creation by AD.EXE?*

1. J:\HOSPITAL
2. J:\HOSPITAL\WPCS
3. J:\HOSPITAL\WPOFFICE
4. J:\HOSPITAL\RADIOLGY
5. J:\HOSPITAL\RADIOLGY\OFFILES
6. J:\HOSPITAL\RADIOLGY\OFUSER

10. *Office 4.0 Options in AD.EXE fails to bring up the Options dialog and displays a "Launcher Program Not Available" error dialog. What program is missing from the installed WordPerfect Office 4.0 files?*

1. AD.EXE
2. WPOPTION.EXE
3. LC.EXE
4. OFSETUP.EXE
5. SETUPOF.EXE
6. SETMEOF.EXE

Multiple-domain systems

11. *Which of the following options will increase message flow performance in domains with a high volume of traffic?*

1. Run multiple message servers for each domain.
2. Run OFS stand-alone for each domain.
3. Run OFS for DOS stand-alone for each post office.
4. Run OFS for OS/2 in an OS/2 window for each post office.

12. *From which of the following networks can you import users from the network directory?*

1. Novell NetWare
2. Banyan STDA
3. IBM LAN Server
4. 3Com 3+
5. LANtastic
6. DEC PCSA
7. LAN Manager
8. NFS

13. *Which of the following considerations will help determine the number of post offices that should be set up in each domain?*

1. The number of file servers on the network.
2. The client software that will be used (DOS, Windows, or Macintosh).
3. The anticipated message traffic between users on different file servers.
4. The network software being used and any limitations that the NOS may impose.

14. *If you plan to have dedicated machines running OFS.EXE for the post offices in your domain, what network rights does the message server (CS.EXE) need in the WPCSOUT directory and its subdirectories on each post office?*

1. Read files
2. Write files
3. Delete files
4. Change file attributes
5. Execute files
6. Supervisory privileges

15. *You have 36 file servers and six message servers with four machines running OFS.EXE. How many domains do you have?*

1. Six domains
2. Five domains
3. Four domains
4. Three domains
5. Two domains
6. One domain

16. *You have just defined a new secondary domain within an existing 4-domain system. All secondary domains have direct links established to the primary domain; however, the message server in domain B doesn't have enough network connections to be able to map a drive to the new secondary domain. What type of link should be defined for domain B's message server to the new domain?*

1. Gateway
2. Indirect
3. Direct
4. None

17. *Why would you want to copy the message server files from the domain/WPCS directory to the hard drive of the message server machine and run it from there?*

1. Running a message server from the local hard drive is often faster than running from the network.
2. Running a message server from the local hard drive is required in order to run stand-alone OFS stations.
3. When running a message server from the local hard drive, it will continue to process messages for post offices in the domain even if the file server where the domain is located goes down.
4. When running a message server from the local hard drive, the PC running the message server does not need access to the domain directory.
5. Running a message server from the local hard drive does not provide any advantages.

18. *When installing the client software from the disks, what must be entered as the destination directory?*

1. The domain directory.
2. The WPOFFICE subdirectory.
3. The post office directory.
4. A local hard drive.
5. Any network directory.

19. *From which of the following networks can you import users into your WordPerfect Office system?*

1. Banyan VINES
2. DEC Pathworks
3. Microsoft LAN Manager
4. Novell NetWare
5. Artisoft LANtastic

20. *Which of the following fields are mandatory when creating a user?*

1. User ID
2. First Name
3. Last Name
4. Department
5. Network ID
6. Acct ID

21. *You have just defined a secondary domain within your system and need to establish the connection between the secondary domain and your primary domain. The message server within the secondary domain can map a drive to the server where the primary domain is located. What is the most efficient type of link you can define in Message Server Network Links for this connection?*

1. Gateway
2. Indirect
3. Direct
4. None

22. *You have just defined a new secondary domain within your system. Which of the following steps are necessary in order to establish the connections from this new secondary domain to the primary domain?*

1. Exit the primary domain's message server and restart it.
2. Define network links from the secondary domain to the primary domain.
3. Rebuild the CSI file for the new domain.
4. Create the objects that currently exist in the primary domain in the new domain.
5. Start the new domain's message server.

23. *What is the maximum number of characters allowed in a post office name?*

1. There is no limit
2. 32 characters
3. 26 characters
4. 8 characters
5. 3 characters

24. *You need to import a user list from a network that is not on the import list in the administration program. Which of the following alternatives could you use to get this list of users into your system?*

1. Enter the names manually.
2. Use the generic network option, and make adjustments as necessary.
3. Put the list into a Secondary Merge File and then into a WordPerfect Office Notebook file.
4. Convert the list to ASCII format and import.

25. *Which of the following can you use to import a user?*

1. ASCII Text File
2. IBM LAN Server
3. Windows for Workgroups
4. Banyan STDA
5. LANtastic
6. Novell NetWare bindery
7. WordPerfect Office Notebook
8. MS LAN Manager

26. *A new employee based in Europe wants to be added to your WordPerfect Office 4.0 system. The affiliate is concerned about the possibility of scheduled appointments being off by several hours. Which of the following options, when set properly in the post office definition, will prevent this from happening?*

1. Directory Exchange
2. Directory Propagation
3. Time Zones
4. Directory Synchronization
5. Network Links

27. *Which of the following are reasons for creating and updating the USERID.FIL?*

1. Help DOS client to locate a user if necessary.
2. Help Windows client to locate a user if necessary.
3. Helps other WordPerfect network applications with FID's.
4. Help maintain a link with WordPerfect Office 3.1.

28. *Which of the following databases can be validated from a secondary domain's AD.EXE?*

1. This secondary domain's domain database.
2. The post office databases in this secondary domain.
3. The primary domain's domain database.
4. The post office database in the primary domain.
5. The post office databases in another secondary domain.

29. *A user in domain 1 sends a high-priority message to a user on post office A in domain 2. In what directory will domain 1's message server place the file so that domain 2's message server can process it?*

1. posta\WPCSIN\2
2. posta\WPCSOUT\OFS\2
3. dom2\WPCSIN\2
4. dom2\WPCSOUT\OFS\2
5. dom2\TRANSIN
6. dom1\WPCSOUT\OFS\2

30. *When a status message is being returned to a sender, what database(s) is/are updated by OFS in the sender's post office?*

1. USERxxx.DB
2. MSGxxxx.DB
3. WPHOST.DB
4. WPUSER.DB

31. *What does it mean if you go into AD.EXE and a post office in the domain is "closed?"*

1. Users cannot get into Office on the post office.
2. Messages cannot be delivered to the post office by the message server.
3. AD.EXE does not have access to the post office WPHOST.DB file.
4. The post office has exceeded the total number of messages possible.

32. *When you add an object for a post office in a secondary domain from that secondary domain's AD.EXE, how is the information about the object replicated throughout the WordPerfect Office 4.0 system?*

1. If the administrator has direct network access to all of the domains in the system, then AD.EXE writes the changes to each domain's database and each domain updates its own post offices the next time AD.EXE is run.
2. AD.EXE updates its domain database and the post office databases in its domain, then generates a message to all of the other domains about the update.
3. AD.EXE updates its domain and post office databases, then sends a message to the primary domain. The primary domain then updates its databases and passes a message about the change to all of the other domains.
4. AD.EXE sends a message to the primary domain about the pending change, the primary domain verifies that it is not a duplicate and sends it back to the secondary domain. Then the change is added in the secondary domain and messages are passed to all of the other domains.
5. The replication will not happen unless the objects are added from the primary domain's AD.EXE.

33. *What is the purpose of the file placed in the domain\WPCSIN\0 directory when the message server CSI file is rebuilt?*

1. To indicate to the domain administrator that the CSI file has changed.
2. To tell the domain administrator what network links have been changed.
3. To tell the message server to reboot.
4. To tell the message server to reinitialize.

34. *What are the consequences of not defining network links from the primary domain to all of the secondary domains in a system?*

1. The message server will return an error message to the user trying to send messages to other domains.
2. The message server will send back an undeliverable status.
3. The message server will report the other domains as being "blocked."
4. Messages cannot be delivered to the primary domain from the secondary domains.

Multiple systems (integrating Office 4.X and 3.X systems)

For the following questions, assume that you are administering a WordPerfect Office system for a company with multiple sites spread throughout the country. The HQ office is in Iowa, and there are branch offices in California (CA), Virginia (VA), and Texas (TX). The company uses WordPerfect Office 3.1 and 4.0.

35. *You are planning to connect the CA WordPerfect Office 3.1 system with the HQ WordPerfect Office 4.0 system. Which of the following is true about the transfer host name?*

1. It must be the WordPerfect Office 4.0 post office name.
2. It must be the WordPerfect Office 4.0 domain name.
3. It must be a valid WordPerfect Office 3.1 host name.
4. It must be a unique name within the WordPerfect Office 3.1 system.

36. *A message was sent from the HQ domain to a user in the VA domain. The TX domain's message server placed the message file in VA domain's WPDOMAIN\WPCSIN\0-7 directory. What type of network link exists between the HQ and VA domains?*

1. Direct
2. Indirect
3. Gateway
4. None

37. *Why is an indirect link less efficient than other link types?*

1. An indirect link requires the message to pass through at least one more message server than a direct link requires.
2. The local domain's message server moves messages through more directories requiring more file I/O.
3. The message server is required to pull more directories for the presence of files when an indirect link is specified.
4. Indirect links increase the number of mapped drives the local domain message server requires for successful mail delivery.
5. The message server's polling cycle time is increased for each indirect link defined within the domain.

38. *A message was sent from the HQ domain to a user in the VA domain. The TX domain's message server placed the message file in VA domain's WPDOMAIN\WPCSIN\0-7 directory. What type of network link exists between the TX and VA domains?*

1. Direct
2. Indirect
3. Gateway
4. None

39. *A message has been sent from a WordPerfect Office 4.0 user to a WordPerfect Office 3.1 user. The message server has picked up the converted file from the WPCSIN directory on the 4.0 domain. Select the directory in which the file is placed next. (Refer to Fig. P4-6.)*

1. A
2. B
3. C
4. D
5. E
6. F
7. G
8. H

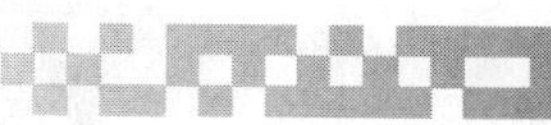

40. *In which directory does the 3.1 connection server place a message being sent from a WP Office 3.1 user to a WordPerfect Office 4.0 user? (Refer to Fig. P4-6.)*

1. A
2. B
3. C
4. D
5. E
6. F
7. G
8. H

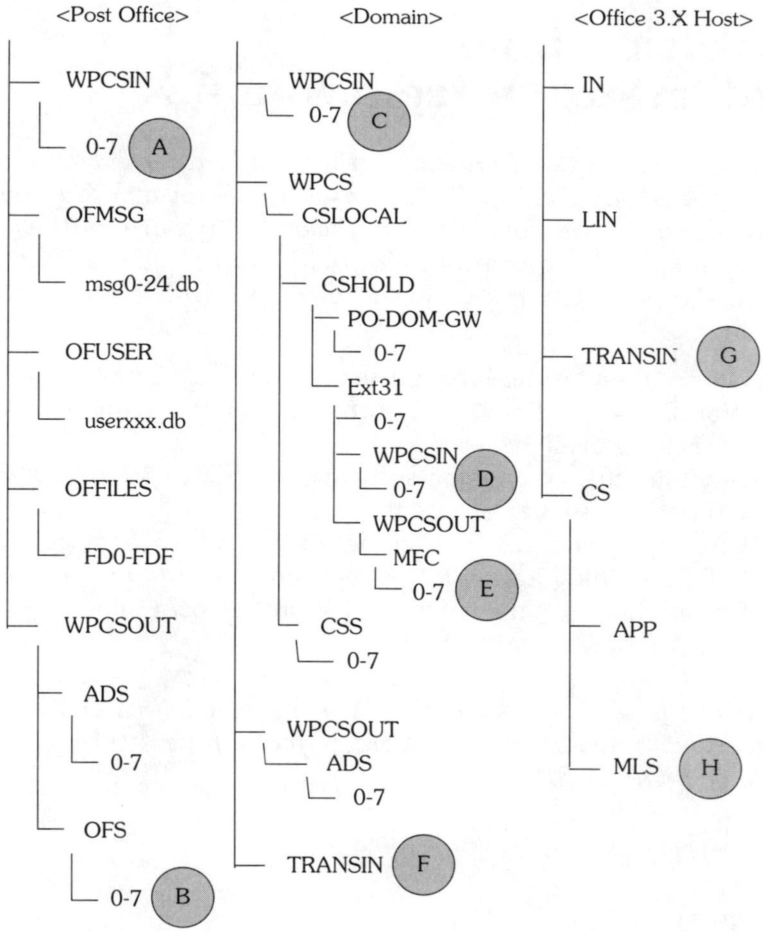

Figure P4-6

<Post Office>
WPCSIN
0-7 A
OFMSG
msg0-24.db
OFUSER
userxxx.db
OFFILES
FD0-FDF
WPCSOUT
ADS
0-7
OFS
0-7 B

<Domain>
WPCSIN
0-7 C
WPCS
CSLOCAL
CSHOLD
PO-DOM-GW
0-7
Ext31
0-7
WPCSIN
0-7 D
WPCSOUT
MFC
0-7 E
CSS
0-7
WPCSOUT
ADS
0-7
TRANSIN F

<Office 3.X Host>
IN
LIN
TRANSIN G
CS
APP
MLS H

41. *A VA user's message did not arrive for the intended CA user. Which directories would you check to find out where the message has stopped? (Refer to Fig. P4-6.)*

1. A
2. B
3. C
4. D
5. E
6. F
7. G
8. H

Conversion from WordPerfect Office 3.X to 4.X

42. *The department you are converting to WordPerfect Office 4.0 is running the WordPerfect Office EasyLink Gateway. You have learned that a 4.0 version of this gateway is currently not available from WordPerfect Corporation. How will you provide immediate access to the 3.1 EasyLink gateway for your WordPerfect Office 4.0 users?*

1. Do not convert the WordPerfect Office 3.1 users to WordPerfect Office 4.0 until the 4.0 version of the EasyLink gateway is available.
2. Buy the MFC conversion software that allows WordPerfect Office 4.0 users to access the 3.1 EasyLink gateway.
3. Use an external 3.1 domain definition to provide access to the 3.1 EasyLink gateway for your WordPerfect Office 4.0 users.
4. Define the 3.1 gateway in your WordPerfect Office 4.0 system as a 4.0 gateway.

43. *Currently, which of following WordPerfect Office Gateway(s) are directly supported by both WordPerfect Office 4.0 and WordPerfect Office 3.1?*

1. MCI
2. AT&T EasyLink
3. Async
4. SMTP
5. X.400

44. *Which of the following is the correct syntax for a complete WordPerfect Office 4.0 address?*

1. System.Domain.PostOffice.UserID
2. System.PostOffice.UserID
3. Domain.PostOffice.UserID
4. PostOffice.UserID@Domain
5. PostOffice.UserID

45. *Which of the following factors will affect the amount of time needed to convert a WordPerfect Office 3.1 system to WordPerfect Office 4.0?*

1. The number of WordPerfect Office 3.1 users to convert.
2. The performance of the machine running the conversion.
3. The performance of the network user's workstations.
4. The number of hosts to convert in the WordPerfect Office 3.1 system.
5. The number of post offices in the WordPerfect Office 4.0 system.

46. *Which of the following is true about SETUPOF.EXE?*

1. It allows NOTIFY.EXE to be installed for individual users.
2. It allows global settings to be defined by the administrator.
3. It requires you to log in as the user for whom you intend to make changes.
4. It allows you to convert calendar files.
5. It allows you to define default settings for users, such as display, location of files, etc.

47. *Which of the following actions should be taken when a post office database becomes corrupted?*

1. Synchronize the post office with the primary domain.
2. Rebuild the post office from its domain database.
3. Restore a backup copy of the post office directory structure and contents.
4. Run OFCHECK.EXE for the post office.

48. *Which of the following addressing methods are correct when sending a message from a WordPerfect Office 4.0 user to a WordPerfect Office 3.1 user?*

1. Domain.post office.user
2. Post office:user
3. Post office:post office:user
4. Post office:domain.post office.user

49. *Your company has just upgraded to WordPerfect Office 4.0. The company wants to continue using Async to communicate with a remote installation of WordPerfect Office 3.1. What must be done so these systems can communicate?*

1. Define a 4.0 Async gateway in WordPerfect Office 4.0 to connect to the WordPerfect Office 3.1 host.
2. Use the existing 3.1 Async Bridge in an external 3.1 system.
3. Define a 3.1 Async Bridge in the new WordPerfect Office 4.0 system.
4. There is no way to connect the two locations.

⇨ WordPerfect Office Remote and gateways

50. *When configuring the Async gateway, the Remote to Async connection type performs which of the following functions?*

1. Enables WordPerfect Office Remote 4.0 users to call in and access their home mailbox.
2. Enables remote Async sites to connect with each other.
3. Provides remote LAN access when using the Async gateway.
4. Provides the capability of connecting to your home mailbox via any third-party communication software.

51. *Before you can define an Async connection to another WordPerfect Office 4.0 system, what information must you have about the other system's Async gateway?*

1. Phone Number
2. Network Operating System
3. Gateway Login Password
4. Domain Name
5. Gateway Login ID

52. *Which of the following are features of the WordPerfect Office Remote to Async gateway connection?*

1. Many remote users can use the same Async gateway connection.
2. Multiple phone lines can be used by the Async gateway connection.
3. The connection will not allow any user direct access to the network.
4. The remote user can download any file from the server.
5. WordPerfect Office Remote 4.0 can call another remote user's laptop when the user has messages to download.

53. *For which of the following can the "Direct Connect" option be used?*

1. Connecting two Async communication servers via a null modem cable.
2. Connecting two Async communication servers using two modems and a dial up line.
3. Connecting two Async communication servers using a leased data line.
4. Connecting two Async communication servers using a direct gateway.

54. *The Async communication server at a remote office has gone down. When a user at the central office sends a message to a user at the remote office, what message will the sender see displayed in the information screen for this message?*

1. Pending
2. Undeliverable
3. Undefined Post Office
4. Undefined User
5. Postponed

Answers to sample questions

WordPerfect 6.0 DOS answers

1. 4. Reasoning: File names cannot be the same as the directory name in which they exist.

2. 1, 2, 3, 4, 8. Reasoning: In the path statement, C: is the hard disk drive. The first \ is the root directory. BUSINESS is the directory and LETTERS is its subdirectory. SMALL.BUS is the file name.

3. 3. Reasoning: Display Pitch does not actually format these options; it only works *with* these options.

4. 2. Reasoning: Shell uses conventional and expanded memory areas for its workspace. The swap files cannot be placed in the HMA or UMB areas. The extended memory area was designed for swap files.

5. 2. Reasoning: If you press Alt-F12 Envelope while in Document Initial Codes, nothing appears on the screen. You can insert any other formatting feature in Document Initial Codes.

6. 3, 4, 5, 7. Reasoning: Headers, footers, and watermarks are all attached to a paragraph when Autocode Placement is active. Tab will always be inserted at the cursor position, whether or not Autocode Placement is active.

7. 3. Reasoning: If the heading is not blocked, only the paragraph style will format it correctly.

8. 1, 2. Reasoning: Only paragraph and character styles are able to Display Off Codes.

9. 2, 3, 5. Reasoning: By definition, a hard return ends a paragraph and is therefore not an option. A Paragraph style can only link to another Paragraph style.

10. 2. Reasoning: Adjust Text is designed to adjust where text prints on the page if the text does not print at the specified margins. You can use a text adjustment to shift the text up, down, left, and right.

11. 2, 3, 5, 6, 7.

12. 2. Reasoning: In 6.0, the first line of text will print over the table line just below it. In 5.x, the text did not print at all.

13. 1. Reasoning: Named ranges can begin with an underscore (_), an alpha character, or any extended character. Except for the first character, a name might include alphanumeric characters, spaces, extended characters, #, $, ?, @, or _ (underscore). Cell names cannot be the same as cell addresses.

14. 2, 4. Reasoning: TTY is a Terminal Emulation type and is not an Application Programming Interface. CAS is an Application Programming Interface that is supported by WordPerfect. FAXDIR is a CAS-interpreting TSR, not an Application Programming Interface. FAXBIOS is an Application Programming Interface that is supported. ANSI is a standardized screen controller used in modem communications and is not an Application Interface. CASMGR is an interpreter for FaxBios commands used by Intel fax boards and is not an Application Programming Interface.

15. 4. Reasoning: PORTUTIL.COM is a utility that is shipped with WordPerfect 6.0 that will give the following information: com port connections, IRQ interrupts, and memory information.

16. 2, 3. Reasoning: You can place a bookmark at the beginning of blocked text. When you return to the bookmark, the text is automatically blocked again.

17. 1. Reasoning: A QuickMark is a generic bookmark. You can only have one QuickMark in a document at a time. If you place a second QuickMark in the document, the first one will be deleted.

18. 2. Reasoning: The document must contain at least one bookmark in order to use the jump feature of Hypertext. You can move between two links in a document, but you cannot jump to another link.

19. 4. Reasoning: To execute a Hypertext link when Hypertext is not active, the cursor must be between the Hypertext link codes.

20. 1. Reasoning: Computers and printers interface through a *port*. If the proper port is not selected, the computer cannot send the information to the printer. The printer port must be set up in the Edit Printer Setup dialog box.

21. 3. Reasoning: You can unmark graphics font types in the Graphics Fonts Data Files dialog box (for example, everything but TrueType graphics fonts) if you do not want that type to display in the Select Graphics Fonts dialog box or in the Font list box.

22. 3, 4. Reasoning: Text and Graphics Quality are document-specific and are saved with the document in the prefix. When that document is exited, F7-Save, Exit-No, and the Text and Graphics Quality options are reset back to defaults for new documents. Number of Copies is set back to default each time you close the current document.

23. 1, 2. Reasoning: If you select WordPerfect, WordPerfect creates the number of copies you specified, and then sends them to the printer, one complete copy at a time. If you select Printer,

WordPerfect sends one copy of the print job to the printer, and the printer generates the number of copies you have specified. The copies are not collated. If you select Network, the network will send the number of copies you have specified to the printer, one complete copy at a time.

24. 2, 4, 5, 7. Reasoning:

- "Copy con com1" is not in postscript language.
- Sending Ehandler.ps to the printer tells the printer that you would like a printout of any future errors that it comes across.
- To see the "COM Port" settings in WP, you must go into Select Printer¦Edit¦Port and select a COM port. The settings in here must match the settings on the printer menus.
- Resetting the paper tray will help, if it wasn't inserted properly.

25. 1, 3, 4, 6, 7, 8. Reasoning:

- The printer is off line, which means that there is power to the printer, but it is not ready to receive data from the computer.
- The printer is out of paper. A laser printer has sensors that detect when it is out of paper to prevent toner from being placed on the drum; therefore, when the paper tray is empty, it will not print.
- Wrong port is selected. If the wrong port is selected in WordPerfect, the computer will not know were to send the data. If a printer is connected to the incorrect port, it will print to that printer. Also, if the port is incorrectly selected, WordPerfect will report that the printer is not accepting data; check the cable and make sure that the printer is turned on in control printer.

26. 1, 4. Reasoning: WordPerfect will only use Conventional and Expanded Memory as workspace. Extended memory can only be used with file caching, swapping files, and loading the WP.FIL file high. WordPerfect can use the UMB only for storing about 6K of temporary files.

27. 3. Reasoning: The only way a paragraph style could be added to a Button Bar would be to create a macro to turn on the style and then assign that macro to a Button Bar. A paragraph style without a macro cannot be added to a Button Bar.

28. 2. Reasoning: Most macros created in WordPerfect 5.1 will correctly convert to 6.0. Any 5.1 macro that uses a combination of cursor movements to select Paper/Size, Font, Styles codes, and the like will not properly convert to 6.0. The Macro Conversion Utility has no way of knowing which Font was two positions down on the screen when the original macro was created.

29. 2. Reasoning: Having an ENDRECORD code anywhere in your FORM file will cause the merge to QUIT as soon as it reaches that point. ENDRECORD is a DATA file code.

30. 4. Reasoning: The FIELD() codes are used to specify position and format each field within a record from the data file. Using the syntax "FIELD(3)" would place the third field of the record in that position exactly where the FIELD() code is in the form file, obeying any formatting codes affecting that position in the document.

31. 2. Reasoning: A hyphen (-) is the "through" operator, and semicolon (;) is the "and" operator.

32. 2, 3, 4. Reasoning: WP will use memory if it is available; if not, it will try and use available disk space. Anything freeing up memory or disk space would help prevent memory errors.

33. 4. Reasoning: If the Table Position is set to Left, the table will come in as it is and print over any text that might be in other columns. If you want it to automatically adjust to the column width, the Table Position must be set to Full.

34. 2. Reasoning: Decreasing the brightness of the graphic will accomplish this task.

35. 2. Reasoning: Attaching a graphic box to a paragraph will allow the box to move up and down on the page as text is added or removed. The graphic will remain centered on the page.

36. 1, 4. Reasoning: Only Column Borders and Graphic Lines will position the vertical line between the columns.

37. 1. Reasoning: If Auto Code Placement is on and you expand a master document, it will remove any redundant codes it finds. For example, if a Widow/Orphan code is in the master document and some of the subdocuments, Auto Code Placement will leave the code in the master but remove any code that it finds in the subdocuments.

38. 3. Reasoning: Normally, the page numbers in your table of contents look like the page numbers in your document. If you want to change the way the page numbers appear in the table of contents, WordPerfect 6.0 now includes a very easy way to do this. In the Define Table of Contents dialog box, you can select Page Numbering Format and change the numbering in the table of contents to include any desired text, chapter, volume, page, and secondary page numbers.

39. 1, 3, 4, 5, 7, 9. Reasoning: You can cross-reference footnotes and endnotes, pages and secondary pages, counters, paragraphs, chapters, volumes, outlines, figures, and captions for graphics boxes.

40. 1, 2, 4. Reasoning: Each list is only capable of generating captions for one type of graphic box. It does not alter capitalization in any way as Index Headings do.

41. 1, 2, 4. Reasoning: While in the Go To dialog box, you need to enter the page number that you want to move the cursor to. If you have multiple occurrences of the same page, as in this question, you must also specify the volume number and chapter number before the page number. If you want to go to the first page of a specific chapter, you do not have to enter the page number because the cursor goes to the first page in that chapter automatically.

42. 2, 3, 4. Reasoning: Some of the areas that will be searched by the extended search feature are headers and footers, graphic box captions, comments, footnotes and endnotes, text boxes, and Table of Authorities Full Forms.

43. 1. Reasoning: Only the code [Open Style:Initial Codes] is present. This cannot be deleted either.

44. 1, 3, 5. Reasoning: When adding words to a supplemental dictionary, you can choose to skip, replace, or offer alternatives to the added word. If you choose to replace the word, you can choose whether or not you want WP to prompt you each time it finds that word during a spell check instead of replacing it automatically. In this example, you can add ABCG to your supplemental dictionary and have WP replace with ABC Graphics. Then go to Speller¦Setup and enable Prompt on Auto-replace.

45. 3. Reasoning: Every WP60 document contains a unique Document Dictionary in the document prefix. The Document Dictionary contains all the words that are skipped during spell check by choosing "Skip in this Document." Words that are added during spell check are saved to the Supplemental Dictionary. The Document and Supplemental Dictionaries can be edited in Speller¦Edit Supplemental Dictionary.

46. 1, 3, 4, 5. Reasoning: Grammatik's predefined Writing Styles are set to one of three formality levels: Informal, Standard, or Formal. The styles Business Letter, Report, Technical, and Proposal all use Formal as their default formality. The other Writing Styles do not require the high level of formality that these styles use.

47. 2. Reasoning: Grammatik allows a user to insert error messages directly into a document. This is one type of Checking that Grammatik can perform. The user should understand that both Mark and Unmark are part of Grammatik's Checking feature.

48. 3. Reasoning: You must first retrieve a document in Grammatik before you can replace one of the standard references in Comparison Charts. Once you have retrieved the document, you can then go into Customize Charts and select the current document to replace one of the standard references.

49. 2, 6, 7, 8. Reasoning: Redline Method can be Alternating Left and Right, Left, Right, and Printer Dependent. You have the option

to choose the method you wish to use either by document in Format¦Document or changing it permanently in Print Setup.

50. 3. Reasoning: When performing a compare document, one document must be on screen and the other document must be on disk; the location does not matter. WP provides a field where you can enter the path and filename of the document to compare.

51. 3. Reasoning: File manager can display the contents of only one directory at a time.

52. 1, 3, 4.

53. 1. Reasoning: Undo restores text in its original location.

54. 1, 2, 3.

55. 2. Reasoning: When printing was stopped, WordPerfect did not record the page number of the last page printed. Printing would resume from the beginning of document only.

56. 1. Reasoning: Lowercase letters are placed before uppercase letters.

WordPerfect 6.0 for Windows answers

1. 2.

2. 4.

3. 4.

4. 3.

5. 2, 3.

6. 1.

7. 2.

8. 1, 2.

9. 2.

10. 3.

11. 3.

12. 5, 6.

13. 3.

14. 2.

15. 1, 4.

16. 1, 2, 3, 4.

17. 2.

18. 1, 4, 5.

19. 2, 5.

20. 6.

21. 3.

22. 2.

23. 4, 7.

24. 1, 3.

25. 3.

26. 5.

27. 2.

28. 2, 3, 5.

29. 1.

30. 1.

31. 1.

32. 2, 3, 4.

33. 1.

34. 2.

35. 4.

36. 4.

37. 1, 2, 3, 5, 6.

38. 2.

39. 3.

40. 1, 4.

41. 5.

42. 6.

43. 3, 5.

44. 2, 4.

45. 3.

46. 1, 2, 3.

47. 2.

48. 1, 3, 7.

49. 1, 2.

50. 2.

InForms answers

1. 3. Reasoning: The (OR) operator is the pipe: ¦.

2. 1. Reasoning: The only way to e-mail your Report information with the form is to export it as an .ML file from the Query screen. (WordPerfect InForms asks if you want to include the Report information.) You can e-mail the database, but all of the links in your form will be incorrect, so when the user tries to fill it in, he or she will receive several error messages. The other options do not exist.

3. 2, 5. Reasoning: You must have the AND operator (comma) to find all of the names greater than M and less than R. The OR operator (pipe) will find records that are greater than M *or* less than R. If you don't have a comma or pipe, you will receive the error message "Query Parse Error."

4. 1. Reasoning: Query uses the Primary Update link first.

5. 1. Reasoning: At least one Form Object *must* be linked to both databases in order to create a Join in Query.

6. 2. Reasoning: Change calculations are executed when any Object changes value. As the value within the Object changes, the Change calculation is executed.

7. 3. Reasoning: Save As Locked lets you save a locked version of a form. Locked forms can be opened in Filler, but not in Designer. This feature prevents users from changing the form.

8. 4. Reasoning: Using the Custom Data Format, you can specify the format in which you enter data. To allow the user to enter only numeric digits, you should use [#].

9. 2, 3, 4. Reasoning: You can lock the tab order of objects to have the user fill in the form in a certain order. The cursor returns to the next item in sequence when a user attempts to move focus out of sequence. The mouse cannot move focus to the next Object when the previous one is not filled in; however, Tab will let you move from Object to Object in the proper order, even if it is not filled in.

10. 4. Reasoning: The New method assigns a number to the record when a form is opened. If the data is not saved, the value is discarded. By selecting Add as the Auto-Increment method, the incremental value does not appear when users fill in the form but is added when the record is saved to a database. This method ensures that each consecutive value is used.

11. 1, 3. Reasoning: Shared Code shipped before WordPerfect InForms is not compatible with WordPerfect InForms. WordPerfect Presentations is a newer shared code and is compatible with WordPerfect InForms. WordPerfect Office 4.0 uses the same shared code as WordPerfect InForms. WordPerfect 6.0 DOS shared code is not compatible with WPCorp for Windows products.

12. 1, 2, 3. Reasoning: Preferences are stored in the WPFx.INI files. WPDF.INI does not exist.

13. 1. Reasoning:

- c:\informs\database is the default for database files.
- c:\informs is the default for the program files.
- c:\informs\learn is the default for the tutorial files.
- c:\informs\data and c:\windows are not defaults using WordPerfect InForms Standard Installation program.
- c:\informs\forms is wrong.

14. 1, 4, 5. Reasoning:

- ➢ FFWIN.EXE executes the FFWINFIL.EXE, which is the program.
- ➢ FDWIN.EXE executes Designer, not Filler.
- ➢ FFQELIB.DLL does not exist.
- ➢ WPFFUS.DLL contains the help prompts and menu text for Filler.
- ➢ WP{FF}.FFD contains the default Button Bar used in Filler.

15. 2. Reasoning: WordPerfect InForms is offered in two separate packages. The Designer package includes the Designer, Filler, and Security applications. A Filler package is also offered, which includes only the Filler application. When using the Designer package installation disks, you cannot choose to install only the Filler application. You must install all of the WordPerfect InForms Program Files and then delete the Designer and Security files. There is no FINSTALL.EXE file included in the installation disks.

16. 1. Reasoning: By default, all WordPerfect Corporation product shared-code files go to C:\WPC.

17. 2, 3, 5, 6, 8. Reasoning: E-mail packages supported by WordPerfect InForms include WordPerfect Office 3.1 and 4.0, cc:Mail 1.1 or later, MS Mail 3.0 or later, and Microsoft Windows for Workgroups Mail or any MAPI-based e-mail system.

18. 4, 5. Reasoning: It does not matter what directory Shared Code files are installed to as long as the user has access to it. Shared Code can only be read from one directory.

19. 1, 3. Reasoning: A user must have access to the Security Database and be listed in a linked approval group. Both .WPF and .ML files can be signed.

20. 1, 3, 4, 5. Reasoning: You cannot install Security separately.

21. 1. Reasoning: The "Access Denied" error occurs when temporary files cannot be created. The /d startup option redirects temporary files.

22. 2, 4. Reasoning: Only .ML files can store data collected via InForms.

23. 1, 2. Reasoning: The Security feature of WordPerfect InForms prevents unauthorized users from altering and/or viewing protected data within WordPerfect InForms.

24. 3. Reasoning: The record is not protected when saving because you can save a record without signing it. It is not protected when only the password matches the Security Database because it still requires you to enter a user ID and vice versa. Only after both the password and the user ID match what is in the Security Database does the record become protected for authentication.

25. 3. Reasoning: Setting up an Approval Group with only one member, then restricting the Signature Field to only that Approval Group, allows only that member to sign the form. The manager in this situation could not just have the highest Level within an Approval Group because Levels cannot be restricted within Designer.

26. 1, 3. Reasoning: The User's ID can default to be the user's password. This can be done in either one of two places. By checking the Default Password Box in either the Add User screen or the Security Preference Options, any user added thereafter will have his or her User ID as a password.

27. 2. Reasoning: You can delete the users and re-create them; however, when you delete a user from the Security Database, any forms that the user signed in the past will no longer pass authentication. Another option is to leave the old user and just add a new one. You can never change or look up a user's password. You cannot copy information from an old user file into a new one.

28. 4. Reasoning: The only way to delete a department is to change to the Department View and delete from there. You cannot delete a department from the Edit User Record screen. There is no Clear option under the Edit menu.

Office answers

1. 3. Reasoning: Whenever you have more than one post office, you must have a message server to link the post offices together. By having one post office that everyone accesses, there is no need to link additional post offices with a message server.

2. 4. Reasoning:

1. Users never write to the domain directory because they do not need any rights there. Users do need all rights, except Supervisor rights, in everything but the root directory of their post office. They only need read rights to the root of the post office.
2. See #1. A user never accesses the message server directory structure; therefore, he or she does not need any rights to this area.
3. See #1.
4. This is the correct answer.
5. See #1.
6. See #1.

3. 1, 2, 3, 5. Reasoning:

1. Running multiple copies of OFS allows each copy of OFS to pick up a message and begin processing it, while the other copies are working processing messages. This decreases the load on the message server.
2. This allows the executables to process much faster.
3. The message server uses either extended or expanded memory to store and process temporary files.
4. Message servers are established for domains, not for individual post offices.

5. Running multiple copies of OFS allows each copy of OFS to pick up a message and begin processing it, while the other copies are working processing messages. The OS/2 OFS application is able to run multiple threads, which provides simultaneous processing on a single machine.

4. 1, 5, 6. Reasoning:

- Yes answer #1: From the message server's point of view, if it cannot locate or "see" the post office with which communication is intended, then it cannot deliver mail.
- Yes answer #2: When message delivery is set to Server Never, it will not deliver messages between post offices.
- Yes answer #3: If the message server is not running, then messages cannot be transferred from one post office to another. The message server will accomplish this.

5. 1. Reasoning: The WPDOMAIN.CSI is located in the domain directory.

6. 4. Reasoning: A U in the Administration Location of Files screen indicates that the user has been locked out of changing this option.

7. 4, 5. Reasoning: The administrator can lock a user's Archive Directory location in the AD.EXE program. The administrator can lock the options for all users on a post office or a single user.

8. 2. Reasoning: The Office program will off load messages to the message server whenever the number of affected databases (sender's plus recipient's) exceeds the application threshold set in the Office 4.0 Options in AD.EXE.

9. 4. Reasoning: The userid.fil file is always placed in the post office directory.

10. 3. Reasoning: LC.EXE is the launcher program that AD.EXE uses to launch OFSETUP.EXE. OFSETUP.EXE is the Office 4.0 Options program.

11. 3, 4. Reasoning: To increase message flow performance, run OFS on its own dedicated machine (DOS or OS/2).

12. 1, 2, 3, 7. Reasoning: This option is selected from the network import feature within AD.EXE.

13. 1, 3, 4. Reasoning: When planning for the number of post offices within a domain, you will need to consider the number of file servers and how many post offices you will have on each (if more than one). If you have post offices that will have users that will send a lot of mail between themselves, put those post offices in the same domain. Some network operating systems limit the number of concurrent attachments to file servers.

14. 1, 2, 3. Reasoning: When you have separate, dedicated machines running OFS.EXE, those machines need read, write, and delete privileges in the WPCSOUT/x directories because OFS is the program that actually processes messages in those directories. CS.EXE (Message Server) only places files in these directories for OFS to process; therefore, it only needs read and write access.

15. 1. Reasoning: There is a one-to-one correlation between the number of domains and message servers.

16. 2. Reasoning: An indirect link should be used because the message server cannot map a drive to the new domain, and it already has a direct link to the primary domain.

17. 1, 3. Reasoning: Running applications from a local drive is often faster because the executable is not loaded across the network. Also, running a message server from a local drive allows it to continue to have access to all of its executable files and working directories, even if all of the servers in the domain are down. As long as a message server has access to its working directories and executables, it will continue to poll and try to reconnect to blocked post offices and domains.

18. 1. Reasoning: You must specify the domain directory during the installation of the client software. The installation program will place

the client software in the WPOFFICE/OFDOS40 (for the DOS client) or WPOFFICE/OFWIN (for the Windows client) directory.

19. 1, 3, 4. Reasoning: Only the following networks are supported for importing users from the network directory: Novell, Banyan, and MS LAN Manager (IBM LAN Server). From other networks, the administrator must either manually import the users or export from the network to an ASCII file, then import that file using AD.EXE.

20. 1. Reasoning: The User ID field is the only field that is mandatory when filling out a user record in AD.EXE. This is different from Office 3.1, where first name and last name were also mandatory.

21. 3. Reasoning: A direct link type requires a network connection from the message server to the domain to which the message server is linking. A direct link is also more efficient than an indirect link because a message traveling through an indirect link must pass through at least one more message server than when going through a direct link.

22. 2, 3, 5. Reasoning: The steps necessary to establish connections from a new secondary domain to the primary domain (and any other domains in the system) are:

1. Define the network links from the secondary domain to all other domains and the links from the existing domains to the new domain.
2. Rebuild the CSI files in each domain. This will automatically restart the message servers in the existing domains; thus, there is no need to manually restart.
3. Start the new domain's message server. Users do not need to exist in the new domain in order for the links to be established.

23. 2. Reasoning: A post office name can be up to 32 characters in length.

24. 1, 3, 4. Reasoning: There is no generic network option. Each of the other alternatives are valid.

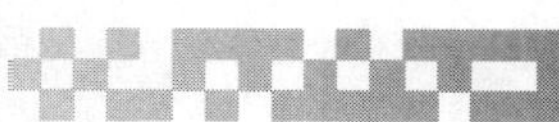

25. 1, 2, 4, 6, 7, 8. Reasoning: WordPerfect Office 4.0 supports the following import options: WordPerfect Office Notebook, ASCII Text File, Novell NetWare bindery, Banyan STDA, IBM LAN Server, and MS LAN Manager.

26. 3. Reasoning: The only option that would affect the time of a mail message or scheduled appointment would be setting the appropriate time zone for each post office.

27. 2, 3. Reasoning: The Windows client will use it if it cannot find the user and then finds the USERID.FIL. A USERID.FIL file in a WordPerfect Office 4.0 post office directory will not influence the sending of mail between WordPerfect Office 3.1 and WordPerfect Office 4.0 systems.

28. 1, 2. Reasoning: The only databases that can be validated from the secondary domain are the secondary domain database and the post office databases in the secondary domain. You can't access databases in the primary domain directly from the secondary domain's AD.EXE.

29. 3. Reasoning: The message server for domain 1 has direct network access to the domain directory in domain 2, and files destined for domain 2's message server from other domains are placed in domain 2's WPCSIN\x directory, where "x" denotes the priority (2=high).

30. 2. Reasoning: Statuses are kept in the sender's MSGxxxx.DB file in the OFMSG directory on the post office.

31. 3. Reasoning: A post office showing up as "closed" means that AD.EXE doesn't have direct network access to the post office at that time. The post office is still fully functional, and if objects are added or changed on that post office, AD.EXE sends a message to the message server and ADS.EXE performs the updates to the WPHOST.DB.

32. 3. Reasoning: AD.EXE in the secondary domain updates its own WPDOMAIN.DB and the WPHOST.DB files for the post offices in its domain and places a message in the domain\WPCSIN\2 directory

destined for the primary domain. The message server moves the message to the primary domain where ADS.EXE updates the primary domain database and all post office databases in the primary domain, then it places a message in the domain\WPCSIN\2 directory destined for all other domains in the system, where (in those domains) the message server and ADS.EXE update their respective domain and post office databases.

33. 4. Reasoning: The file placed in the domain\WPCSIN\0 directory when the CSI file is built is routed to the message server, where the CSS process reads the file and reinitializes the message server. The message server will then reread the CSI file and know about its new configuration.

34. 3. Reasoning: Messages sent to a domain for which the message server has no network links defined will be stored until the network links are established. The user will not be informed of a problem; he or she will not receive a status back.

35. 2, 3, 4. Reasoning: The transfer host name can be any valid unique WP Office 3.1 host name. Whatever name you choose must be entered into the "Return Domain Name" field for the WordPerfect Office 4.0 direct link to the 3.1 system; however, it is recommended that the transfer host name be the same as the WordPerfect Office 4.0 domain name to which you are connecting.

36. 2. Reasoning: The message servers in and between WordPerfect Office systems must be connected, whether by a gateway or directly. Since the message was placed into the TX domain's WPCSIN directory, the network link between HQ and VA is an indirect link via TX.

37. 1. Reasoning: An indirect link does not require the domain's message server to have a physical network connection to the other domain directory. It uses the existing direct links of an adjacent domain. Indirect links can only be used with three or more domains.

38. 1. Reasoning: The message servers in and between WordPerfect Office systems must be connected, whether by a gateway or directly. Because the message was placed into the domain's WPCSIN directory, the network link is a direct link.

39. 6. Reasoning: After the message server has picked up the file and MFC has converted it, the message server places the file in the TRANSIN directory under the WordPerfect Office 3.1 host, where the 3.1 connection server picks it up and delivers it.

40. 6. Reasoning: Answer: TRANSIN in 4.0 domain directory.

41. 1, 4, 5, 7, 8. Reasoning: The chronological order of directories a message file is placed in when it is being moved from a 4.0 user to a 3.1 user is as follows:

1. <PO>\WPCSIN\<0–7>
2. CSHOLD\<EXT31>\WPCSOUT\MFC\<0–7>
3. CSHOLD\<EXT31>\WPCSIN\<0–7>
4. 3.1 Host TRANSIN
5. 3.1 Host CS\MLS

42. 3. Reasoning: For a WordPerfect Office 4.0 system to route messages to a WordPerfect Office 3.1 gateway, you must have a functional 3.1 system, including a Connection Server, running the 3.1 gateway. You would then define this system as an External 3.1 domain in your 4.0 AD program and route messages that need to go out the 3.1 gateway through this domain. You do not need to have users defined on your 3.1 system.

43. 3, 4, 5. Reasoning: Using the WordPerfect Office 4.0 release (7/93) there is an Async gateway, X.400 Gateway, and SMTP Gateway for both Office 3.1 and 4.0. Use of the X.400 requires an OS/2 station in Office 4.0. The SMTP Gateway is supported from the Unix platform and requires the use of Office 3.1 for Unix. The MCI and AT&T EasyLink gateways are supported by WordPerfect Office 3.1. (Contact WordPerfect Corporation for the latest information on available gateways: 801-226-6944.)

44. 3. Reasoning: A WordPerfect Office 4.0 user's address is made of three elements. The first element is the name of the user's domain. The second element is the name of the user's post office. The third element is the User ID of the user. All three elements

together make up the unique ID for each user on the Office 4.0 system.

45. 1, 2, 4. Reasoning: The number of hosts and users in the WordPerfect Office 3.1 system is a large factor in the amount of time that it will take to convert the system to WordPerfect Office 4.0. The performance of the WordPerfect Office 4.0 administration machine is also a factor; the faster the machine and the faster its link to the network, the faster the conversion can happen.

46. 1, 4. Reasoning: The purpose of SETUPOF.EXE is to configure individual user workstations for running WordPerfect Office 4.0, including installing NOTIFY.EXE into the user's AUTOEXEC.BAT files. SETUPOF.EXE also converts a user's WordPerfect Office 3.1 calendar files and archive folders to 4.0 format.

47. 2. Reasoning: Rebuilding the post office database re-creates it using the information from its domain.

48. 1, 2. Reasoning: WordPerfect Office 4.0 can use either domain.post office.user (or post office.user) or post office:user.

49. 2. Reasoning: Remember that some gateways that exist in WordPerfect Office 3.1 systems will need to be left online and used even after WordPerfect Office 4.0 is installed. In this case, the 4.0 Async gateway will not communicate with a 3.1 Async Bridge. In order to preserve the communication between the new WordPerfect Office 4.0 system and the WordPerfect Office 3.1 system asynchronously, you will need to communicate via a 3.1 to 3.1 Async connection and indirectly link the new 4.0 system to the 3.1 system via an intermediate 3.1 host and Async Bridge.

50. 1. Reasoning: A "Remote to Async" connection is designed to allow WordPerfect Office Remote users to connect to the home Office 4.0 system. Only the WordPerfect Office Remote program will have access.

51. 1, 3, 5. Reasoning: The following information is required when defining an Async gateway connection: Phone number, Gateway Login Password, Gateway Login ID.

52. 1, 2, 3. Reasoning: The WordPerfect Office Remote to Async Gateway connection will allow many users to call in to the connection. In addition, multiple phone lines can be set up on each of the connections. The users call in to send or receive their messages. The remote user cannot download a file by just using the Async gateway. Remote users cannot dial and connect with another WordPerfect Office Remote user.

53. 1, 3. Reasoning: A "Direct Connection" can be achieved when using a null modem cable (in place of a modem) or when using a leased data line.

54. 1. Reasoning: When the Async communication server is not operational, messages that must be sent through the Async gateway will sit in a queue directory. The message will have a pending status until the message is delivered to its destination.

Appendices

Certification checklists

APPENDIX A

We hope that the following checklists will come in handy when trying to prepare for the different exams. You should spend a reasonable amount of time on the different topics. You may study by using the practice materials and the study guides, or just working with the product.

Use the space next to each topic in the section column to make notes about questions or problems that you encounter when working with that feature. Under "time studied," make notes about the amount of time spent studying on that topic. Under "score/questions," write your score from the practice exam. If you developed your own questions, make a note about how many were related to this topic and how many questions you answered correctly.

WordPerfect Office 4.0 Exam CSE

Section	Time Studied	Score/Questions
Planning		
Installation		
Maintenance		
Troubleshooting		
Conversion		
ASYNC gateway		
Office remote		
Generic gateway		

WordPerfect InForms 1.0 Exam CPC

Section	Time Studied	Score/Questions
Query & Report		
Distribution		
Calculations		
Links		
Form layout		

WordPerfect InForms 1.0 CSE

	Time Studied	Score/Questions
System Administration:		
Security		
Network system		
Stand-alone machine		
Creation, distribution, and use of forms:		
Query and report		
Distribution		
Calculations		
Links		
Form layout		

WordPerfect 6.0 for DOS CPC

	Time Studied	Score/Questions
Setting Up WordPerfect		
Managing files		
Formatting documents		
Editing documents		
Automating tasks		
Professional publications		
Tables/spreadsheets		
Special features		
Printing		
Troubleshooting		

B

Important telephone numbers

CompuServe accounts
800-848-8990

Computer Shopper subscription
800-274-6384

Drake Training and Technology
800-2WP-EXAM
800-297-3926

Novell
800-233-3382

SpaceWorks Online Support
800/5-SPACE-5
800-577-2235

Sylvan Learning Centers
800-869-1100

WordPerfect after-hours support (all products)
801-222-9010

WordPerfect BBS IBM (9600 baud/V.32)
801-225-4444

WordPerfect BBS IBM (1200/2400 baud)
801-225-4414

WordPerfect BBS Macintosh
801-226-1605

WordPerfect BBS Support (Voice Only)
801-228-9904

WordPerfect BBS UNIX
801-228-9909

WordPerfect Certification Department
800-993-3700

WordPerfect Certification Information Center
(To request that a list of certification training centers and instructors be mailed to you.)
800-321-3260

WordPerfect Certification Fax Information Center
(To request that a list of certification training centers and instructors be faxed to you; request FAX document number 2001.)
801-228-9921

WordPerfect Corporation (conferences fax information)
800-321-3240
801-228-5050

WordPerfect Information, General
800-451-5151
801-225-5000

WordPerfect InfoShare Faxback Service
800-228-9960
801-228-9920

WordPerfect Magazine Subscription Services
801-228-8804

WordPerfect Orders
800-321-4566
801-226-6800

WordPerfect Registration
801-222-4555

WordPerfect Report
801-225-5000

WordPerfect Reseller Feedback
800-321-0034

WordPerfect Software Subscriptions
800-282-2892
801-226-6800

WordPerfect Update Information Hotline
800-321-5906
801-226-4444

WordPerfect Workgroup Expert Newsletter
801-228-9626

Glossary

.ALL (WordPerfect) A file that contains information about currently configured printers.

.CSI (Office) WordPerfect Office message server configuration file.

.INI A file type that stores Windows startup and configuration information.

.LEX (WordPerfect) Main dictionary file for use with speller.

.ML (InForms) A form-document file extension associated with moving the file over a network connection.

.PRS (WordPerfect) A file that contains information about a specific configured printer.

.SDB (InForms) Security database file format extension.

.WPF (InForms) WordPerfect InForms format file extension.

.WPG WordPerfect graphics format file extension.

ACTS Association of Computer Training and Support Professionals.

ADMIN (Office) The Office administration program. The filename of this program is AD.EXE.

appearance (WordPerfect) The appearance of a font refers to the font displays **BOLD**, *ITALIC*, and UNDERLINE, or a combination of these features.

application A computer program such as WordPerfect, InForms, or Office/GroupWise.

asynchronous gateway (Office/GroupWise) A software program and associated hardware that links two Office/GroupWise domains or a remote user (or users) to a domain.

ATA Authorized Training Associate.

ATC Authorized Training Center.

ATEC Association of Technical Education Centers.

BBS A dial-up bulletin board system that allows you to send and receive messages and files. Requires the use of a modem.

BIOS Basic Input and Output System. A computer program that resides on a chip inside a PC that instructs the PC how to start up.

button bar A feature of WordPerfect products that allows the user to associate a graphic image with a command or macro. The button bar is used by positioning the mouse over the bar and pressing one of the mouse buttons.

causal A type of question that seeks to determine the cause of something, or determining why something happens.

CBC Certified Business Credential.

certified partner Someone who is a WordPerfect CBC, CPC, CSE, ECSE, or CI.

CI Certified Instructor.

CIS CompuServe Information Service.

CNEPA Certified NetWare Engineers Professional Association (now called the NPA, or Network Professional Association).

Coaches (WordPerfect) A special macro feature that instructs a user how to complete a complicated operation.

CompuServe An online information service.

conversational Information that can be exchanged by talking.

conversion The process of changing a file in one format to another format.

courseware A package that contains all course materials including a workbook and a reference book and possibly software.

CBC Certified Business Credential.

CPC Certified Professional Credential.

CR Certified Resource. CR is a form of certification in a previous WordPerfect certification program.

credential Evidence that you have met certain predefined requirements. WordPerfect views the certifications that it confers on people as credentials.

CSE Certified System Engineer.

customer support The service provided by a company to the people who purchase and use its products.

DataPerfect WordPerfect Corporation's database product.

distracter Used to refer to an answer in a multiple-choice question that looks like it could be correct, but is incorrect.

domain (Office) The main administration unit of a WordPerfect Office system.

Drake Drake Certification Testing. A company that delivers the WordPerfect certification exams.

DTP Desktop publishing.

ECSE Enterprise Certified System Engineer.

educator A person who teaches at a school, institute, or college.

email Electronic mail allows a LAN user to send a message to another user on the LAN. If the other user is not at a computer, the mail is delivered the next time that he or she uses the network.

essential skills The knowledge people should have about computers before they get involved with the training or certification program.

Folio (Folio Corporation) An online information system used to access WordPerfect technical support information on CD-ROM.

form designer (InForms) Used to create new forms.

form filler (InForms) Used to complete or fill in forms that were created using the designer.

gateway (Office) A system that transfers messages into or out of a WordPerfect Office domain specifically between incompatible systems or environments.

Grammatik WordPerfect grammar-checking software product.

GroupWise (Novell GroupWise) New name for the WordPerfect Office 4.0 electronic mail, calendar, and schedule application.

GUI Graphical user interface.

Hard Disk Cafe The company cafeteria at WordPerfect headquarters in Orem, Utah.

Hypertext A system of links that allows a reader to jump to different locations in a document.

InfoBase WordPerfect CD-ROM support database.

InForms WordPerfect forms design and management product.

InfoShare WordPerfect fax-back system.

job analysis Process of determining how a person accomplishes a task.

LAN Local Area Network.

landscape Page orientation where the width is greater than the height.

link Using InForms, a link is a connection between two objects.

macro A type of computer program that is written using commands of a particular software product. Macros allow a series of commands to be executed as one.

master document (WordPerfect) A feature that allows the user to compose a large document from several smaller documents.

menu bar The area at the top of a window containing the heading for pull-down menu items.

merge (WordPerfect) A feature that allows a user to create a series of customized documents, such as letters, using data, such as names and addresses, that are stored in a separate file.

message server (Office) A system that routes messages between post offices.

MIDI The musical instrument digital interface is a means for connecting sound-enabled devices to a computer.

multi-multiple choice A multiple-choice question with more than one correct answer.

multiple systems (Office/GroupWise) When Office/GroupWise file servers are linked together by a LAN or other network.

object When using InForms, the object is a line, symbol, or shape that is used in a form.

object library A related group of objects.

Office WordPerfect calender, messaging (mail), and scheduling product.

office server (Office) A type of message server that runs on its own PC.

path The address of a directory or file on a disk.

permanent evaluation software People at certain levels of certification are provided the opportunity to purchase copies of WordPerfect products at a significant discount.

PlanPerfect A WordPerfect spreadsheet product.

port A connector on a PC computer that is used to attach a peripheral device: printer, scanner, modem.

portrait Page orientation where the height is greater than the width.

post office (Office) A collection of related user mail boxes.

POSTNET A type of bar-code system used by postal services to encode zip codes.

power bar A type of button bar.

preferences The setup of a particular user's computer.

prerequisite Something that you need before you attempt to get something else. A knowledge of DOS is a prerequisite for taking the WordPerfect DOS CBC exam.

Presentations A WordPerfect presentation graphics product.

procedural An action accomplished by performing steps in a specific order.

proxy (Office/GroupWise) A feature that allows another user to perform a function in your place.

referral When WordPerfect customer support sends a potential client in a certified person.

remote office (Office/GroupWise) A user located at a remote location would use this software to connect to the network to send or receive email.

satisfaction guarantee WordPerfect requires all certified trainers to offer a satisfaction guarantee that ensures a student will be able to get his or her money back (less the cost of materials provided by the instructor) if not fully satisfied with the training.

shell A menulike interface for DOS computers.

signature (InForms) Approval of a filled-in form document. A user signs a document by adding his or her identification code and password.

Sylvan Sylvan Learning Centers.

SysOps System operators manage a BBS or forum, such as a CompuServe forum.

third-party Third-party products are books or software that you purchase that are not manufactured by WordPerfect but work with or rely on a WordPerfect product.

tool palette (InForms) In a Windows environment, a tool palette is a floating window (or box) with a number of point-and-click tools available for the user. Unlike a button bar, a palette can appear anywhere on the screen.

transitional courseware Teaches a user of a software package other than WordPerfect to use the WordPerfect product based upon commands already known from another product.

user A person who is using a PC that is attached to a network. User ID is the name used to access the network.

vertical market When a company sells products or services only to other companies in a specific industry, that market is referred to as a vertical market.

Watermark A graphic image that appears as a shadow behind the printed text on a page.

wild card A character that can be used to denote another character or characters. The asterisk (*) and question mark (?) are the DOS wild card characters.

WISE strategy The WordPerfect information system environment is WordPerfect Corporation's strategy for integrating a series of products to help a user perform his or her job.

work model The knowledge that a user has that lets him or her complete a task.

WYSIWYG "What You See Is What You Get." What you see on the computer's monitor is what the printer will reproduce.

Index

D

E

F

G

H

I

L

M

N

O

About the authors

This book is based upon Brian Ford's and Debra Kiefer-Ford's experiences operating a computer consulting business. They have helped a wide range of clients, from Fortune 500 companies to small one-person firms, meet today's challenges through the use of business computer software. The Fords have supported and trained users on WordPerfect products for seven years, while also training on many other software applications.

Clients have included all skill levels, from beginner to near-expert. The Fords have trained on a one-to-one basis and for large groups.

Debra Ford holds an A.S. degree in computer science from Suffolk County Community College. She is a technical coordinator for a large school district. Debra first became involved in the WordPerfect certification program in 1990 when she became a certified resource and then a certified instructor.

Brian Ford holds a B.S. degree in computer science from the State University of New York at Stony Brook. He is a training manager for the North American subsidiary of an international telecommunications firm. In addition to Brian's WordPerfect Office/Novell GroupWise Certified System Engineer credential, he is a Novell Certified NetWare Instructor and Enterprise Certified NetWare Engineer.

Other Bestsellers of Related Interest

Teach Yourself WordPerfect 6
—Mary Campbell
Covers all the basics and newest features. Hands-on 15-minute lessons will get you going fast with the latest release of the top-selling word processing software for IBM and compatible PCs.
0-07-881894-X $24.95 Paper

The Novell CNA/CNE Study Guide
—John Mueller, CNE, and Robert Williams, CNE, CNI
The only Novell certification study guide for both CNE/CNA certifications; written by two CNEs, one of whom is also a Certified NetWare Instructor.
0-07-911904-2 $38.95 Paper

Microsoft Certification Success Guide
—John Mueller
A unique, one-step guide to Microsoft's many certification programs, by a certified expert! Provides essential information for systems engineers, LAN and MIS managers, and others who want to obtain certification in Excel, LAN Manager, Project, Mail, SQL Server, Windows for Workgroups, Windows NT, and Word
0-07-043973-7 $38.95 Paper

WordPerfect for Windows Answers: Certified Tech Support
—Mary Campbell
This reliable, easy-to-follow guide is great for every reader's level of expertise. From deciphering error messages to common graphics pitfalls, from headers to footnotes and everything on the page in between, this book is packed with answers.
0-07-882053-7 $16.95 Paper

WordPerfect 6: The Complete Reference
—Allen Wyatt, Jim Sheldon, and Steven Nameroff
Covers such WordPerfect capabilities as desktop publishing, integrating WordPerfect with other software, and much, much more.
0-07-881901-6 $29.95 Paper

The Best 1001 WordPerfect Tips Ever
—Mary Campbell
Covers indispensable shortcuts and tips that are organized by topic so you can quickly pinpoint the information needed.
0-07-881819-2 $39.95 Paper

WordPerfect 6 Made Easy
—Mella Mincberg
Hands-on lessons and practical applications will have you producing reports and other professional-looking documents in no time.
0-07-881895-8 $24.95 Paper

How to Order

Call 1-800-822-8158
24 hours a day,
7 days a week
in U.S. and Canada

Mail this coupon to:
McGraw-Hill, Inc.
Blue Ridge Summit, PA
17294-0840

Fax your order to:
717-794-5291

EMAIL
70007.1531@COMPUSERVE.COM
COMPUSERVE: GO MH

Thank you for your order!

Shipping and Handling Charges

Order Amount	Within U.S.	Outside U.S.
Less than $15	$3.45	$5.25
$15.00 - $24.99	$3.95	$5.95
$25.00 - $49.99	$4.95	$6.95
$50.00 - and up	$5.95	$7.95

EASY ORDER FORM— SATISFACTION GUARANTEED

Ship to:

Name ______________________

Address ______________________

City/State/Zip ______________________

Daytime Telephone No. ______________________

ITEM NO.	QUANTITY	AMT.
	Shipping & Handling charge from chart below	
	Subtotal	
	Please add applicable state & local sales tax	
	TOTAL	

Method of Payment:

☐ Check or money order enclosed (payable to McGraw-Hill)

☐ Cards ☐ VISA

☐ MasterCard ☐ DISCOVER

Account No. ☐☐☐☐☐☐☐☐☐☐☐☐☐☐☐☐

Signature ______________________ Exp. Date ________

Order invalid without signature

In a hurry? Call 1-800-822-8158 anytime, day or night, or visit your local bookstore.

Code = BC44ZNA